ABORIGINAL REMAINS IN VERDE VALLEY, ARIZONA

LECTOR HOUSE PUBLIC DOMAIN WORKS

ABORIGINAL REMAINS IN VERDE VALLEY, ARIZONA

COSMOS MINDELEFF

ISBN: 978-93-5342-102-1

First Published: -

LECTOR HOUSE LLP
E-MAIL: lectorpublishing@gmail.com

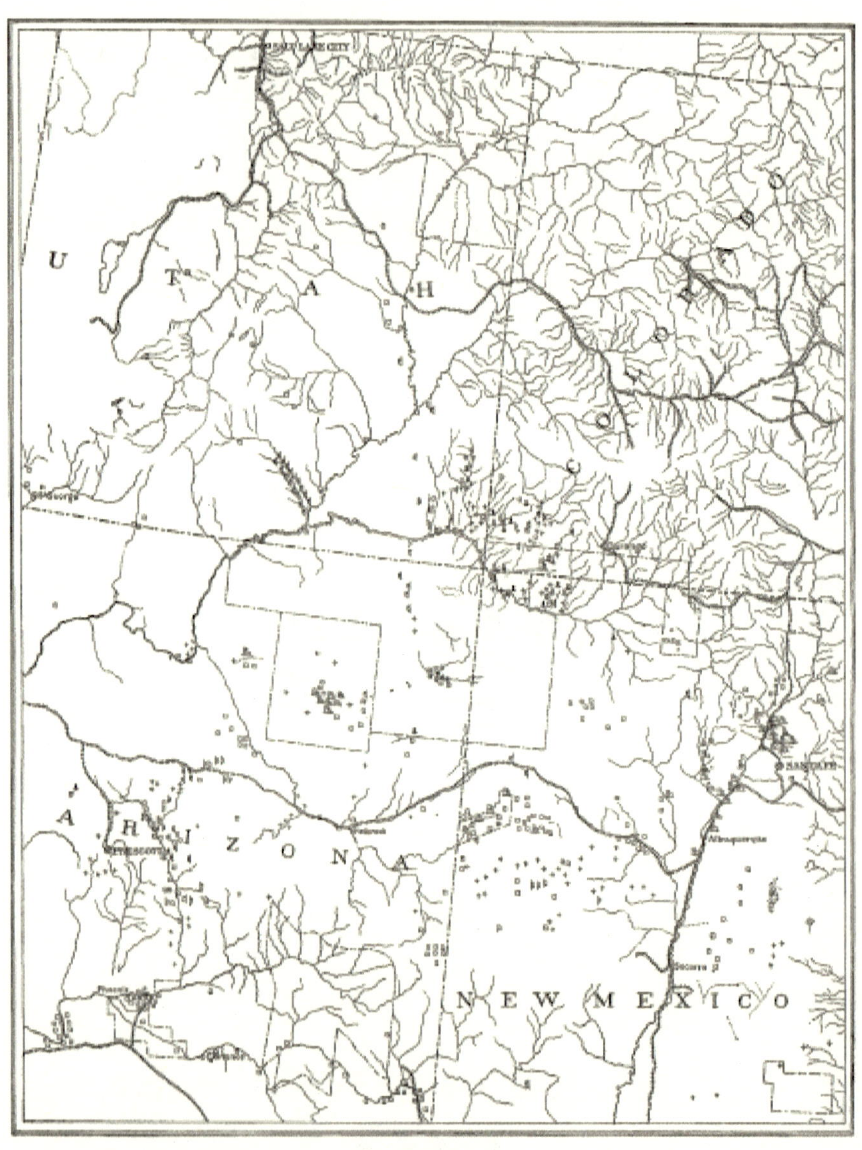

PLATE X. MAP SHOWING DISTRIBUTION OF RUINS AND LOCA-
TION OF AREA TREATED WITH REFERENCE TO ANCIENT PUEB-
LO REGION.

ABORIGINAL REMAINS IN VERDE VALLEY, ARIZONA

BY

COSMOS MINDELEFF

CONTENTS

LIST OF FIGURES

INTRODUCTION.
THE REGION AND ITS LITERATURE.

The region described in the following pages comprises the valley of the Rio Verde, in Arizona, from Verde, in eastern central Yavapai county, to the confluence with Salt river, in Maricopa county.

The written history of the region treated extends back only a few years. Since the aboriginal inhabitants abandoned it, or were driven from it, the hostile Apache and Walapai roamed over it without hindrance or opposition, and so late as twenty-five years ago, when the modern settlement of the region commenced, ordinary pursuits were almost impossible. Some of the pioneer settlers are still in possession, and are occupying the ground they took up at the time when the rifle was more necessary for successful agriculture than the plow.

The first notice of this region is derived from the report of Espejo, who visited some "mines" north and east of the present site of Prescott early in 1583; in 1598 Farfan and Quesada of Oñate's expedition visited probably the same locality from Tusayan, and in 1604 Oñate crossed the country a little way north of the present Prescott, in one of his journeys in search of mineral wealth. Nothing seems to have come of these expeditions, however, and the remoteness of the region from the highways of travel and its rough and forbidding character caused it to remain unknown for over two centuries. It was not until the active prospecting for gold and silver accompanying the American invasion and conquest began that the country again became known. Valuable mines were discovered east and south of the site of Prescott, some of them as early as 1836; but it was not until after 1860 that any considerable amount of work was done, and the mining development of this region, now one of the best known in Arizona, may be said to date from about 1865. Camp Verde was first established in 1861, at a point on the northern side of Beaver creek, but was not regularly occupied until 1866. In 1871 it was removed to its present location, about a mile south of the previous site. It was abandoned as a military post in 1891, and gradually lost the military element of the name.

Concerning the archeologic remains of the Rio Verde valley almost nothing is known. In the early history of Arizona the Verde was known as Rio San Francisco, and vague rumors of large and important ruins were current among trappers and prospectors. The Pacific railway reports, published in 1856, mention these ruins on the authority of the guide to Lieut. Whipple's party, Leroux by name. Other notices are found here and there in various books of exploration and travel published during the next two decades, but no systematic examination of the region was made and the accounts are hardly more than a mention. In 1878 Dr. W. J. Hoffman, at that time connected with the Hayden Survey, published descriptions of the so-called Montezuma well and of a large cliff ruin on Beaver creek, the latter accompanied by an illustration.[1] The descriptions are slight and do not touch the region herein discussed.

The first publication of importance to the present inquiry is a short paper by Dr. E. A. Mearns, U.S. Army, in the Popular Science Monthly for October, 1890. Dr. Mearns was stationed for some years at Camp Verde, and improved the opportunity afforded by numerous hunting expeditions and tours of duty to acquaint himself with the aboriginal remains of the Verde valley. He published a map showing the distribution of remains in that region, described several ruins in detail, and illustrated some pieces of pottery, etc., found by him. The article is unfortunately very short, so short that it is hardly more than an introduction to the wide field it covers; it is to be hoped that Dr. Mearns will utilize the material he has and publish a more comprehensive report.

The remains in the valley of Rio Verde derive an additional interest from their position in the ancient pueblo region. On the one hand they are near the southwestern limit of that region, and on the other hand they occupy an intermediate position between the ruins of the Gila and Salt river valleys and those of the northern districts. The limits of the ancient pueblo region have not yet been defined, and the accompanying map (plate X) is only preliminary. It illustrates the limited extent of our knowledge of the ancient pueblo region as well as the distribution of ruins within that region, so far as they are known; and the exceptional abundance of ruins noted on certain portions of the map means only that those parts are better known than others. Notwithstanding its incompleteness, it is the best available and is published in the hope that it will serve as a nucleus to which further data may be added until a complete map is produced.

The ruins in the Gila valley, including those along Salt river, are less known than those farther northward, but we know that there is a marked difference between the type exemplified by the well-known Casa Grande, near Florence, Arizona, and that of which the best specimens (notably the Chaco ruins) are found in the San Juan basin. This difference may be due only to a different environment, necessitating a change in material employed and consequent on this a change in methods, although it seems to the writer that the difference is perhaps too great to be accounted for in this way. Be the cause what it may, there is no doubt that there is a difference; and it is reasonable to expect that in the regions lying between the southern earth-constructed and the northern stone structures, intermediate types might be found which would connect them. The valley of Rio Verde occupies such an intermediate position geographically, but the architectural remains found in it belong to the northern type; so we must look elsewhere for connecting links. The most important ruin in the lower Verde region occurs near its southern end, and more distinctly resembles the northern ruins than the ruins in the northern part of that region.

Although the examination of this region failed to connect the northern and

[1] Tenth Ann. Rep. U.S. Geol. Survey for 1876 (Washington, 1878), p. 477.

southern types of house structure, the peculiar conditions here are exceptionally valuable to the study of the principles and methods of pueblo building. Here remains of large villages with elaborate and complex ground plan, indicating a long period of occupancy, are found, and within a short distance there are ruins of small villages with very simple ground plan, both produced under the same environment; and comparative study of the two may indicate some of the principles which govern the growth of villages and whose result can be seen in the ground plans. Here also there is an exceptional development of cavate lodges, and corresponding to this development an almost entire absence of cliff dwellings. From the large amount of data here a fairly complete idea of this phase of pueblo life may be obtained. This region is not equal to the Gila valley in data for the study of horticultural methods practiced among the ancient Pueblos, but there is enough to show that the inhabitants relied principally and, perhaps, exclusively on horticulture for means of subsistence, and that their knowledge of horticultural methods was almost, if not quite, equal to that of their southern neighbors. The environment here was not nearly so favorable to that method of life as farther southward, not even so favorable as in some northern districts, and in consequence more primitive appliances and ruder methods prevailed. Added to these advantages for study there is the further one that nowhere within this region are there any traces of other than purely aboriginal work; no adobe walls, no chimneys, no constructive expedients other than those which may be reasonably set down as aboriginal; and, finally, the region is still so little occupied by modern settlers that, with the exception of the vicinity of Verde, the remains have been practically undisturbed. A complete picture of aboriginal life during the occupancy of the lower Verde valley would be a picture of pueblo life pursued in the face of great difficulties, and with an environment so unfavorable that had the occupation extended over an indefinite period of time it would still have been impossible to develop the great structures which resulted from the settlements in Chaco canyon.

It is not known what particular branch of the pueblo-building tribes formerly made their home in the lower Verde valley, but the character of the masonry, the rough methods employed, and the character of the remains suggest the Tusayan. It has been already stated that the archeologic affinities of this region are northern and do not conform to any type now found in the south; and it is known that some of the Tusayan gentes—the water people—came from the south. The following tradition, which, though not very definite, is of interest in this connection, was obtained by the late A. M. Stephen, for many years a resident near the Tusayan villages in Arizona, who, aside from his competence for that work, had every facility for obtaining data of this kind. The tradition was dictated by Anawita, chief of the Pat-ki-nyûmû (Water house gentes) and is as follows:

We did not come direct to this region (Tusayan)—we had no fixed intention as to where we should go.

We are the Pat-ki-nyû-mû, and we dwelt in the Pa-lát-kwa-bĭ (Red Land) where the kwá-ni (agave) grows high and plentiful; perhaps it was in the region the Americans call Gila valley, but of that I am not certain. It was far south of here, and a large river flowed past our village, which was large, and the houses were high, and a strange thing happened there.

Our people were not living peaceably at that time; we were quarreling among ourselves, over huts and other things I have heard, but who can tell what caused their quarrels? There was a famous hunter of our people, and he cut off the tips from the antlers of the deer which he killed and [wore them for a necklace?] he always carried them. He lay down in a hollow in the court of the village, as if he had died, but our people doubted this; they thought he was only shamming death, yet they covered him up with earth. Next day his extended hand protruded, the four fingers erect, and the first day after that one finger disappeared [was doubled up?]; each day a finger disappeared, until on the fourth day his hand was no longer visible.

The old people thought that he dug down to the under world with the horn tips.

On the fifth day water spouted up from the hole where his hand had been and it spread over everywhere. On the sixth day Pá-lü-lü-koña (the Serpent deity) protruded from this hole and lifted his head high above the water and looked around in every direction. All of the lower land was covered and many were drowned, but most of our people had fled to some knolls not far from the village and which were not yet submerged.

When the old men saw Pá-lü-lü-koña they asked him what he wanted, because they knew he had caused this flood; and Pá-lü-lü-koña said, "I want you to give me a youth and a maiden."

The elders consulted, and then selected the handsomest youth and fairest maid and arrayed them in their finest apparel, the youth with a white kilt and paroquet plume, and the maid with a fine blue tunic and white mantle. These children wept and besought their parents not to send them to Pá-lü-lü-koña, but an old chief said, "You must go; do not be afraid; I will guide you." And he led them toward the village court and stood at the edge of the water, but sent the children wading in toward Pá-lü-lü-koña, and when they reached the center of the court where Pá-lü-lü-koña was the deity and the children disappeared. The water then rushed down after them, through a great cavity, and the earth quaked and many houses tumbled down, and from this cavity a great mound of dark rock protruded. This rock mound was glossy and of all colors; it was beautiful, and, as I have been told, it still remains there.

The White Mountain Apache have told me that they know a place in the south where old houses surround a great rock, and the land in the vicinity is wet and boggy.

We traveled northward from Palat-kwabi and continued to travel just as long as any strength was left in the people—as long as they had breath. During these journeys we would halt only for one day at a time. Then our chief planted corn in the morning and the pá-to-la-tei (dragon fly) came and hovered over the stalks and by noon the corn was ripe; before sunset it was quite dry and the stalks fell over, and whichever way they pointed in that direction we traveled.

When anyone became ill, or when children fretted and cried, or the young people became homesick, the Co-i-yal Katcina (a youth and a maiden) came and danced before them; then the sick got well, children laughed, and sad ones became cheerful.

We would continue to travel until everyone was thoroughly worn out, then we would halt and build houses and plant, remaining perhaps many years.

One of these places where we lived is not far from San Carlos, in a valley, and another is on a mesa near a spring called Coyote Water by the Apache.   *   *   *

When we came to the valley of the Little Colorado, south of where Winslow now is, we built houses and lived there; and then we crossed to the northern side of the valley and built houses at Homolobi. This was a good place for a time, but a plague of flies came and bit the suckling children, causing many of them to die, so we left there and traveled to Ci-pa (near Kuma spring).

Finally we found the Hopi, some going to each of the villages except Awatobi; none went there.

PHYSICAL DESCRIPTION OF THE COUNTRY.

The Rio Verde is throughout its length a mountain stream. Rising in the mountains and plateaus bounding two great connected valleys northwest of Prescott, known as Big Chino valley and Williamson valley, both over 4,000 feet above the sea, it discharges into Salt river about 10 miles south of McDowell and about 25 miles east of Phoenix, at an elevation of less than 1,800 feet above the sea. The fall from Verde to McDowell, a distance of about 65 miles, is about 1,500 feet The whole course of the river is but little over 150 miles. The small streams which form the river unite on the eastern side of Big Chino valley and flow thence in a southerly and easterly direction until some 12 miles north of Verde the waterway approaches the edge of the volcanic formation known on the maps as the Colorado plateau, or Black mesa, and locally as "the rim." Here the river is sharply deflected southward, and flows thence in a direction almost due south to its mouth. This part of the river is hemmed in on both sides by high mountain chains and broken every few hundred yards by rapids and "riffles."

Its rapid fall would make the river valuable for irrigation if there were tillable land to irrigate; but on the west the river is hugged closely by a mountain chain whose crest, rising over 6,000 feet above the sea, is sometimes less than 2 miles from the river, and whose steep and rugged sides descend in an almost unbroken slope to the river bottom. The eastern side of the river is also closely confined, though not so closely as the western, by a chain of mountains known as the Mazatzal range. The crest of this chain is generally over 10 miles from the river, and the intervening stretch, unlike the other side, which comes down to the river in practically a single slope, is broken into long promontories and foothills, and sometimes, where the larger tributaries come in, into well-defined terraces. Except at its head the principal tributaries of the Verde come from the east, those on the west, which are almost as numerous, being generally small and insignificant.

Most of the modern settlements of the Rio Verde are along the upper portion of its course. Prescott is situated on Granite creek, one of the sources of the river, and along other tributaries, as far down as the southern end of the great valley in whose center Verde is located, there are many scattered settlements; but from that point to McDowell there are hardly a dozen houses all told. This region is most rugged and forbidding. There are no roads and few trails, and the latter are feebly marked and little used. The few permanent inhabitants of the region are mostly "cow men," and the settlements, except at one point, are shanties known as "cow camps." There are hundreds of square miles of territory here which are never visited by white men, except by "cow-boys" during the spring and autumn round-ups.

Scattered at irregular intervals along both sides of the river are many benches and terraces of alluvium, varying in width from a few feet to several miles, and comprising all the cultivable land in the valley of the river. Since the Verde is a mountain stream with a great fall, its power of erosion is very great, and its channel changes frequently; in some places several times in a single winter season. Benches and terraces are often formed or cut away within a few days, and no portion of the river banks is free from these changes until continued erosion has lowered the bed to such a degree that that portion is beyond the reach of high water. When this occurs the bench or terrace, being formed of rich alluvium, soon becomes covered with grass, and later with mesquite and "cat-claw" bushes, interspersed with such cottonwood trees as may have survived the period when the terrace was but little above the river level. Cottonwoods, with an occasional willow, form the arborescent growth of the valley of the Verde proper, although on some of the principal tributaries and at a little distance from the river groves of other kinds of trees are found. All these trees, however, are confined to the immediate vicinity of the river and those of its tributaries which carry water during most of the year; and as the mountains which hem in the valley on the east and west are not high enough to support great pines such as characterize the plateau country on the north and east, the aspect of the country, even a short distance away from the river bottom, is arid and forbidding in the extreme.

Within the last few years the character of the river and of the country adjacent to it has materially changed, and inferences drawn from present conditions may be erroneous. This change is the direct result of the recent stocking of the country with cattle. More cattle have been brought into the country than in its natural state it will support. One of the results of this overstocking is a very high death rate among the cattle; another and more important result is that the grasses and other vegetation have no chance to seed or mature, being cropped off close to the ground almost as soon as they appear. As a result of this, many of the river terraces and little valleys among the foothills, once celebrated for luxuriant grass, are now bare, and would hardly afford sustenance to a single cow for a week. In place of strong grasses these places are now covered for a few weeks in spring with a growth of a plant known as "filaree," which, owing to the rapid maturing of its seeds (in a month or less), seems to be the only plant not completely destroyed by the cattle, although the latter are very fond of it and eat it freely, both green and when dried on the ground. As a further effect of the abundance of cattle and the scarcity of food for them, the young willows, which, even so late as ten years ago, formed one of the characteristic features of the river and its banks, growing thickly in the bed of the stream, and often forming impenetrable jungles on its banks, are now rarely seen.

Owing to the character of the country it drains, the Rio Verde always must have been subject to freshets and overflows at the time of the spring rains, but until quite recently the obstructions to the rapid collection of water offered by thickly growing grass and bushes prevented destructive floods, except, perhaps, on exceptional occasions. Now, however, the flood of each year is more disastrous than that of the preceding year, and in the flood of February, 1891, the culminating point of intensity and destructiveness was reached. On this occasion the water rose in some places over 20 feet, with a corresponding broadening in other places, and flowed with such velocity that for several weeks it was impossible to cross the river. As a result of these floods, the grassy banks that once distinguished the river are now but little more than a tradition, while the older terraces, which under normal circumstances would now be safe, are being cut away more and more each year. In several localities near Verde, where there are cavate lodges, located originally with especial reference to an adjacent area of tillable land, the terraces have been completely cut away, and the cliffs in which the cavate lodges occur are washed by the river during high water.

DISTRIBUTION AND CLASSIFICATION OF RUINS.

All the modern settlements of the lower portion of the Verde valley are located on terraces or benches, and such localities were also regarded favorably by the ancient builders, for almost invariably where a modern settlement is observed traces of a former one will also be found. The former inhabitants of this region were an agricultural people, and their villages were always located either on or immediately adjacent to some area of tillable soil. This is true even of the cavate lodges, which are often supposed to have been located solely with reference to facility of defense. Owing to the character of the country, most of the tillable land is found on the eastern side of the river, and as a consequence most of the remains of the former inhabitants are found there also, though they are by no means confined to that side. These remains are quite abundant in the vicinity of Verde, and less so between that point and the mouth of the river. The causes which have induced American settlement in the large area of bottom land about Verde doubtless also induced the aboriginal settlement of the same region, although, owing to the different systems of agriculture pursued by the two peoples, the American settlements are always made on the bottom lands themselves, while the aboriginal settlements are almost always located on high ground overlooking the bottoms. Perched on the hills overlooking these bottoms, and sometimes located on the lower levels, there was once a number of large and important villages, while in the regions on the south, where the tillable areas are as a rule very much smaller, the settlements were, with one exception, small and generally insignificant. The region treated in these pages is that portion of the valley of Rio Verde comprised between its mouth and Verde, or Beaver creek, on the north. It was entered by the writer from the south; it is not proposed, however, to follow a strict geographic order of treatment, but, on the contrary, so far as practicable, to follow an arrangement by types.

The domiciliary ruins of this region fall easily into three general classes, to which may be added a fourth, comprising irrigating ditches and works, the first class having two subclasses. They are as follows:

Stone villages.
a. Villages on bottom lands.
b. Villages on defensive sites.

Cavate lodges.
Bowlder-marked sites.
Irrigating ditches and works.

The ruins of the first group, or stone villages located on bottom lands without reference to defense, represent in size and in degree of skill attained by the builders the highest type in this region, although they are not so numerous as those of the other groups. They are of the same type as, although sometimes smaller in size than, the great valley pueblos of the regions on the north and south, wherein reliance for defense was placed in massive and well-planned structures and not on natural advantages of location. In the north this class of ruin has been shown to be the last stage in along course of evolution, and there is a suggestion that it occupies the same relation to the other ruins in the Verde region; this question, however, will later be discussed at some length. The best example of this type on the lower Verde is a large ruin, located in a considerable bottom on the eastern side of the river, about a mile above the mouth of Limestone creek. This is said to be the largest ruin on the Verde; it is certainly the largest in the region here treated, and it should be noted that it marks practically the southern limit of the Rio Verde group.

The ruins of the second subclass, or stone villages located on defensive sites, are found throughout the whole of this region, although the type reaches its best development in the northern portion, in the vicinity of Verde. The separation of this type from the preceding one is to a certain extent arbitrary, as the location of a ruin is sometimes determined solely by convenience, and convenience may dictate the selection of a high and defensible site, when the tillable land on which the village depends is of small area, or when it is divided into a number of small and scattered areas; for it was a principle of the ancient village-builders that the parent village should overlook as large an extent as possible of the fields cultivated by its inhabitants.

A good illustration of this type of ruin is found a little way northeast of Verde, on the opposite side of the river. Here a cluster of ruins ranging from small groups of domiciles to medium-sized villages is found located on knobs and hills, high up in the foothills and overlooking large areas of the Verde bottom lands. These are illustrated later. Another example, also illustrated later, occurs on the eastern side of the river about 8 miles north of the mouth of Fossil creek. The village, which is very small, occupies the whole summit of a large rock which projects into the stream, and which is connected with the mainland by a natural causeway or dike. This is one of the best sites for defense seen by the writer in an experience of many years.

Cavate lodges are distributed generally over the whole northern portion of the region here treated. At many points throughout this region there are outcrops of a calcareous sandstone, very soft and strongly laminated and therefore easily excavated. This formation often appears in the cliffs and small canyons bordering on the streams, and in it are found the cavate lodges. The best examples are found some 8 miles south of Verde, in a small canyon on the eastern side of the river, and it is noteworthy that in this case stone villages occur in conjunction with and subordinate to the cavate lodges, while elsewhere within this region and in other regions the cavate lodges are found either alone or in conjunction with and subordinate to stone villages. To this latter type belong a number of cavate lodges on the northern side of Clear creek, about 4 miles above its mouth. The cavate lodges of the Verde differ in some particulars from those found in other regions; they are not excavated in tufa or volcanic ash, nor are the fronts of the chambers generally walled up. Front walls are found here, but they are the exception and not the rule.

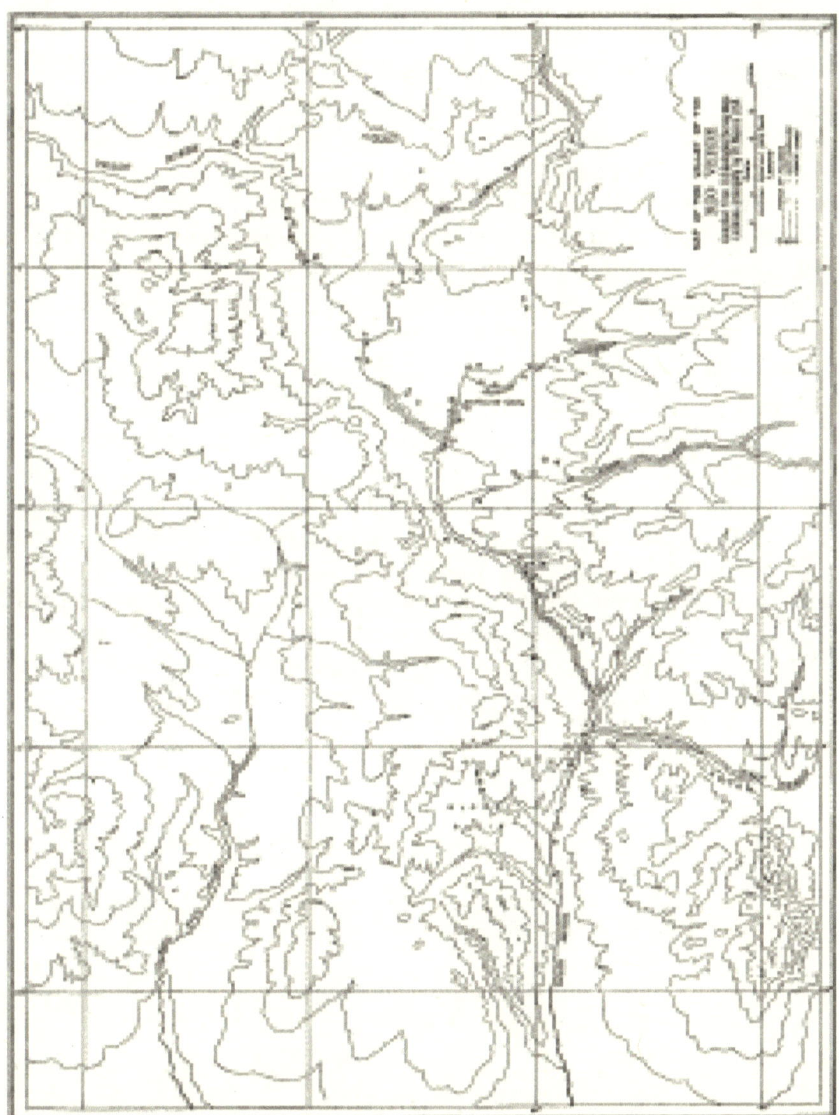

PLATE XI. MAP OF THE VALLEY OF THE RIO VERDE.

Bowlder-marked sites are scattered over the whole region here treated although they are more abundant in the southern part than in the northern. They are so abundant that their locations could not be indicated on the accompanying map (plate XI). These constitute a peculiar type, not found elsewhere in the experience of the writer, and present some points of interest. They vary in size from one room to considerable settlements, but the average size is two or three rooms. They are always located with reference to some area, generally a small one, of tillable land which they overlook, and all the data now available support the inference that they mark the sites of small farming or temporary shelters, occupied only during the farming season and abandoned each winter by the inhabitants, who then return to the main pueblo—a custom prevalent today among the pueblos. These sites are found on the flat bottom lands of the river, on the upper terraces overlooking the bottoms, on points of the foothills, in fact everywhere where there is an area of tillable land large enough to grow a few hills of corn. They often occur in conjunction with irrigating ditches and other horticultural works; sometimes they are located on small hillocks in the beds of streams, locations which must be covered with water during the annual floods; sometimes they are found at the bases of promontories bordering on drainage channels and on the banks of arroyas, where they might be washed away at any time. In short, these sites seem to have been selected without any thought of their permanency.

Irrigating ditches and horticultural works were found in this region, but not in great abundance; perhaps a more careful and detailed examination would reveal a much larger number than are now known. Fine examples of irrigating ditches were found at the extreme northern and the extreme southern limits of the region here treated, and there is a fair presumption that other examples occur in the intermediate country. These works did not reach the magnitude of those found in the Gila and Salt river valleys, perhaps partly for the reason that the great fall of Verde river and its tributaries renders only short ditches necessary to bring the water out over the terraces, and also partly because irrigation is not here essential to successful horticulture. In good years fair crops can be obtained without irrigation, and today this method of farming is pursued to a limited extent.

PLANS AND DESCRIPTIONS.
STONE VILLAGES.

Ruins of villages built of stone, either roughly dressed or merely selected, represent the highest degree of art in architecture attained by the aborigines of Verde valley, and the best example of this class of ruin is found on the eastern side of the river, about a mile above the mouth of Limestone creek. The site was selected without reference to defense, and is overlooked by the hills which circumscribe a large semicircular area of bottom land, on the northern end of which the village was located. This is the largest ruin on the Verde; it covers an area of about 450 feet square, or over 5 acres, and has some 225 rooms on the ground plan. From the amount of debris we may infer that most of the rooms were but one story in height; and a reasonable estimate of the total number of rooms in the village when it was occupied would make the number not greater than 300 rooms. The ratio of rooms to inhabitants in the present pueblos would give a population for this village of about 450 persons. Zuñi, the largest inhabited pueblo, covering an area of about 5 acres, has a population of 1,600.

It will thus be seen that, while the area covered by this village was quite large, the population was comparatively small; in other words, the dense clustering and so-called beehive structure which characterize Zuñi and Taos, and are seen to a less extent in Oraibi, and which result from long-continued pressure of hostile tribes upon a village occupying a site not in itself easily defensible, has not been carried to such an extent here as in the examples cited. But it is also apparent that this village represents the beginning of the process which in time produces a village like Zuñi or Taos.

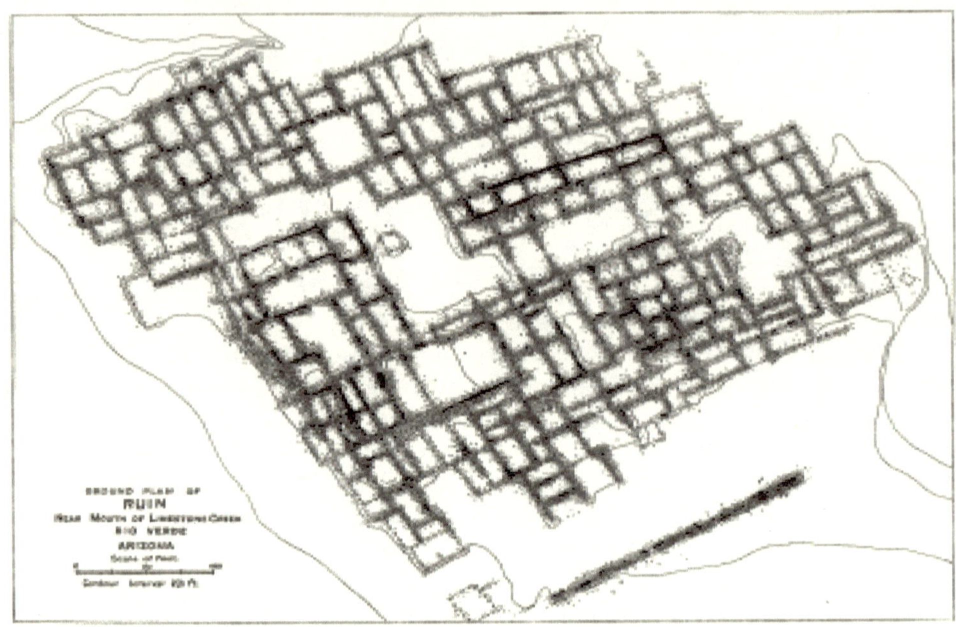

PLATE XII. GROUND PLAN OF RUIN NEAR MOUTH OF LIME-
STONE CREEK RIO VERDE, ARIZONA

Plate XII exhibits the ground plan of the village. It will be observed that this plan is remarkably similar in general characters to the ground plan of Zuñi.[2] A close inspection will reveal the presence of many discrepancies in the plan, which suggest that the village received at various times additions to its population in considerable numbers, and was not the result of the gradual growth of one settlement nor the home of a large group coming en masse to this locality. It has been shown[3] that in the old provinces of Tusayan and Cibola (Moki and Zuñi) the present villages are the result of the aggregation of many related gentes and subgentes, who reached their present location at different times and from different directions, and this seems to be the almost universal rule for the larger pueblos and ruins. It should be noted in this connection, however, that, the preceding statements being granted, a general plan of this character indicates an essentially modern origin or foundation.

The ground plan shows a number of courts or open spaces, which divided the village into four well-defined clusters. The largest court was nearly in the center of the village, and within it (as shown, on the plan) there are traces of a small single-room structure that may have been a kiva of sacred chamber. Attached to this main court and extending eastward is another court of considerable size, and connected with this second court at its eastern end there is another one almost square in plan and of fair size. West of the main court may be seen a small court opening into it, and north of this another square space separated from the main

[2] Eighth Ann. Rep. Bureau of Ethnology, 1886-'87, Wash., 1891, pl. lxxvi.
[3] Ibid., pp. 1-228.

court by a single stone wall and inclosed on the other three sides by rooms. In addition to these there are two completely inclosed small courts in the center of the southwestern cluster, and another one of moderate size between the southwestern and southern clusters.

PLATE XIII. MAIN COURT, RUIN NEAR LIMESTONE CREEK.

The arrangement of these courts is highly suggestive. The central space was evidently the main court of the village at the time of its greatest development, and it is equally evident that it was inclosed at a later period than the small inclosed courts immediately adjacent to it, for had the latter not preceded it they would not occupy the positions they now do. Plate XIII represents a part of the main court, and beyond the débris can be seen a small portion of the bottom upon which the village is built. To the left, in the foreground of the illustration, are traces of a small detached room, perhaps the main kiva[4] of the village; this is also shown on the ground plan, plate XII.

The smaller courts are but little larger than the largest rooms, but it will be noticed that while some of the rooms are quite large they are always oblong. This requirement was dictated by the length of available roofing timbers. The cottonwood groves on the river bank would provide timber of fair size but of very poor quality, and, aside from this, roofing timbers longer than 15 feet could be obtained only at points many miles distant. In either case the hauling of these timbers to the

---

[4] The kiva is the assembly chamber, termed estufa in some of the older writings, particularly those of the early Spanish explorers. A full description of these peculiar structures has already been published in an article on Pueblo architecture; Eighth Ann. Rep. Bureau of Ethnology, 1886-'87, Wash., 1891, pp. 1-228.

site of the village would be a work of great labor and considerable difficulty. The width of the rooms was, therefore, limited to about 20 feet, most of them being under 15 feet; but this limitation did not apply to the courts, which, though sometimes surrounded on all sides by buildings, were always open to the sky.

It is probable that the central and northern portion of the southwestern cluster comprised the first rooms built in this village. This is the portion which commands the best outlook over the bottom, and it is also on the highest ground. Following this the southern cluster was probably built; afterwards the northern cluster was added, and finally the northwestern cluster. Subsequently rooms connecting these clusters and the eastern end of the village were built up, and probably last of all were added the rooms which occupied what was originally the eastern end of the main court. This hypothetic order of building the clusters composing the village is supported by the character of the site and the peculiarities of the ground plan. Most of the rooms in the northwestern cluster and in the eastern part of the village were but one story in height, while the crowding in the interior of the village, direct evidence of which is seen on the ground plan, could take place only after the rooms surrounding that area had been located, and when hostile pressure from outside made it undesirable to extend the bounds of the village; in other words, at the latest stage in the growth of the village.

The arrangement and distribution of the rooms within the clusters indicate an occupancy extending over a considerable period of time. A reference to the ground plan will show that continuous wall lines are the exception, and it is seldom that more than two or three rooms are grouped together in regular order. In irregularity of arrangement the inhabitants of this village followed a general habit, the result of which can be seen today in all the inhabited villages and in most of the large pueblo ruins. It indicates a steady growth of the village by the addition of rooms, one or two at a time, as they were needed. The division into clusters, however, indicates an aggregation of related gentes or subgentes banded together for protection. Given these conditions, (1) bands of related families living near one another; (2) hostile pressure from outside; and (3) a site not in itself easily defended, and a ground plan similar to the one under discussion must result. Single detached rooms would not be built when the village might be attacked at any time, but they might be added during periods of peace and, the conditions being favorable, they might form the nuclei of other clusters. It is possible that some of the clusters forming this village had their origin in this manner, but this question can not be determined from the ground plan, as a similar result would be produced by the advent of a small band of related families.

Growth in number of rooms does not necessarily indicate growth in population, and this qualification must not be lost sight of in the discussion of pueblo ground plans. Among the Pueblos of today, descent, in real property at least, is in the female line; when a man marries he becomes a member of his wife's family and leaves his own home to live with his wife's people. If the wife's home is not large enough to contain all the members of the household, additional rooms are built adjoining and connected with those previously occupied. It may be mentioned in this connection that the women build the houses, although the men supply the material and do the heavy work. The result of this custom may be readily seen: a family in which there are many daughters must necessarily increase the space occupied by it, while a family consisting of sons, no matter how many they may be, will become extinct, so far as regards its home in the village. It is no uncommon thing to see in the villages of today several rooms in course of erection while there are a dozen or more rooms within a few steps abandoned and going to decay. Long occupancy, therefore, produces much the same effect on a ground plan of a village as a large population, or a rapidly growing one, except that in the former case irregularity in the arrangement of rooms will be more pronounced.

It will be noticed that the size of rooms is more varied in the southwestern and southern clusters than in the remaining portions of the village. In the southwestern cluster rooms measuring 8 feet by 18 or 20 are not uncommon. These occur principally in the central and southwestern part of the cluster, while in the northern and northeastern part the rooms are uncommonly large, one of them measuring about 40 feet in length by nearly 15 feet in width and presenting a floor area of 600 square feet. Rooms approaching this size are more common, however, in the northern and northwestern clusters. In these latter clusters long narrow rooms are the exception and a number of almost square ones are seen. The smallest room in the village is in the center of the southern cluster, on the highest ground within the area covered by the ruin; it measures 6 feet by 10, with a floor area of 60 square feet, as opposed to the 600 square feet of the largest room. This small room was probably at one time a small open space between two projecting rooms, such as are often seen in the inhabited pueblos. Later the room on the south was built and the front of the space was walled up in order to make a rectangular area, thus forming the small room shown on the ground plan. The maximum length of any room is about 40 feet, the maximum width attained is about 20 feet, and in a general way it may be stated that the average size of the rooms is considerably larger than that of the rooms in the northern ruins.

From the regularity in distribution of the debris now on the ground, it appears that the rooms of the northwestern and northern clusters, including the eastern part of the village, were almost uniformly one story in height, and most of the rooms in the other clusters were also limited in height to a single story. The only places on the ground plan where rooms of two stories might have existed are the northern and central parts of the southwestern and southern clusters, and perhaps the southern side of the northern cluster; the last, however, being very doubtful.

In the scarcity of detached rooms or small clusters the plan of this village strongly resembles the ground plan of Zuñi. Only three detached rooms are seen in the plan. One of these, situated in the main or central court, has already been referred to as probably the remains of a kiva or sacred chamber. Another single room occurs outside of the village, near its southwestern corner. This was probably a dwelling room, for a kiva would hardly be located in this place. The third room is found also outside the village and at its southeastern corner. The space inclosed within the walls of this room measured about 7 feet by 4 and the lines of wall are at an acute angle with the wall lines of the village. This structure is anomalous, and its purpose is not clear.

The absence of clearly defined traces of passageways to the interior of the village is noticeable. This absence can hardly be attributed to the advanced state of decay in the ruin, for nearly all the wall lines can still be easily traced. At one point only is there a suggestion of an open passageway similar to those found in the inhabited pueblos. This occurs in the southeastern corner of the ground plan, between the southern cluster and the southern part of the northeastern cluster. It was about 25 feet long and but 6 feet wide in the clear. There were undoubtedly other passageways to the interior courts, but they were probably roofed over and perhaps consisted of rooms abandoned for that purpose. This, however, is anomalous.

There are several other anomalous features in the ground plan, the purposes of which are not clear. Prominent among them is a heavy wall extending about halfway across the southern, side of the village and at some distance from it. The total length of this wall is 164 feet; it is 4 feet thick (nearly twice the thickness of the other walls), and is pierced near its center by an opening or gateway 4 feet wide. The nearest rooms of the village on the north are over 40 feet away. This wall is now much broken down, but here and there, as shown on the plan, portions of the original wall lines are left. It is probable that its original height did not exceed 5 or 6 feet. The purpose of this structure is obscure; it could not have been erected for defense, for it has no defensive value whatever; it had no connection with the houses of the village, for it is too far removed from them. The only possible use of this wall that occurs to the writer is that it was a dam or retaining wall for a shallow pool of water, fed by the surface drainage of a small area on the east and northeast. There is at present a very slight depression between the wall and the first houses of the village toward the north—about a foot or a foot and a half—but there may have been a depression of 2 or 3 feet here at one time and this depression may have been subsequently filled up by sediment. This conjecture could be easily tested by excavating a trench across the area between the wall and the houses, but in the absence of such an excavation the suggestion is a mere surmise.

Another anomalous feature is found in the center of the southwestern cluster. Here, in two different rooms, are found walls of double the usual thickness, occurring, however, on only one or two sides of the rooms. These are clearly shown on the ground plan. The westernmost of the two rooms which exhibit this feature has walls of normal thickness on three of its sides, while the fourth or eastern side consists of two walls of normal thickness, built side by side, perhaps the result of some domestic quarrel. The eastern room, however, has thick walls on its northern and eastern sides, and in this case the walls are built solidly at one time, not consisting, as in the previous case, of two walls of ordinary thickness built side by side. An inspection of the ground plan will show that in both these cases this feature is anomalous and probably unimportant.

A ruin of the same general type as that just described, but much smaller in size, is found about 6 miles farther northward on the eastern side of the river. It is located on the river edge of a large semicircular flat or terrace, near its northern end, and is built of flat slabs of limestone and river bowlders. It is rectangular in plan and of moderate size. On the southern end of the same flat are two single-room rancher's houses and a large corral. The rooms in this ruin are oblong and similar in size and arrangement to those just described.

About 11 miles above the last-described ruin, or 17 miles above the large ruin near Limestone creek, there is another small ruin of the same general type as the last, located on a similar site, and in all respects, except size, closely similar to it.

About 3 miles below the mouth of the East Verde there is still another ruin of similar character, located on the edge of a mesa or bench overlooking the river. It is built of bowlders and slabs of rock. Like the others this ruin is rectangular in plan and of small size.

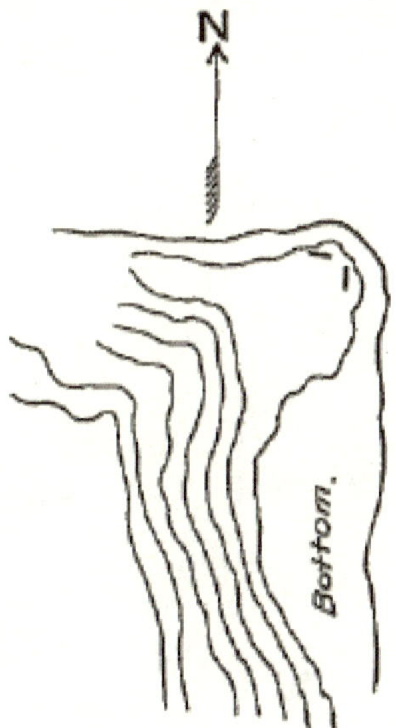

FIG. 279.—SKETCH MAP, SITE OF SMALL RUIN 10 MILES NORTH OF FOSSIL CREEK.

About 10 miles north of the mouth of Fossil creek, on the point of a bench or terrace on the western side of the river, and perhaps 20 feet above it, occurs a small ruin, similar in character to the preceding. The river here makes a long turn eastward, then flows south again, and in the angle a small bench or terrace is formed. At this point the mountains rise abruptly from the river on both sides to a height of over a thousand feet. Fig. 279 illustrates the location of this ruin. So far as could be distinguished from the hills opposite, the rooms occur in two broken lines at right angles to each other.

These four small ruins are all closely similar to the large ruin described above in all respects except size, and peculiarities of ground plan attendant on size. The rooms are always rectangular, generally oblong, and arranged without regularity as regards their longer axis. Except the one last described, the ruins consist of compact masses of rooms, without evidences of interior courts, all of very small size, and all located without reference to defense. The last-described ruin differs from the others only in the arrangement of rooms. There is practically no standing wall remaining in any of them, and even now they can be seen for miles from the hills above. When the walls were standing they must have been conspicuous landmarks. The masonry of all consists of flat bowlders, selected doubtless from the river bed, or perhaps sometimes quarried from the terraces, which themselves contain large numbers of river bowlders. In general appearance and in plan these ruins resemble the ruin next to be described, situated near the mouth of the East Verde.

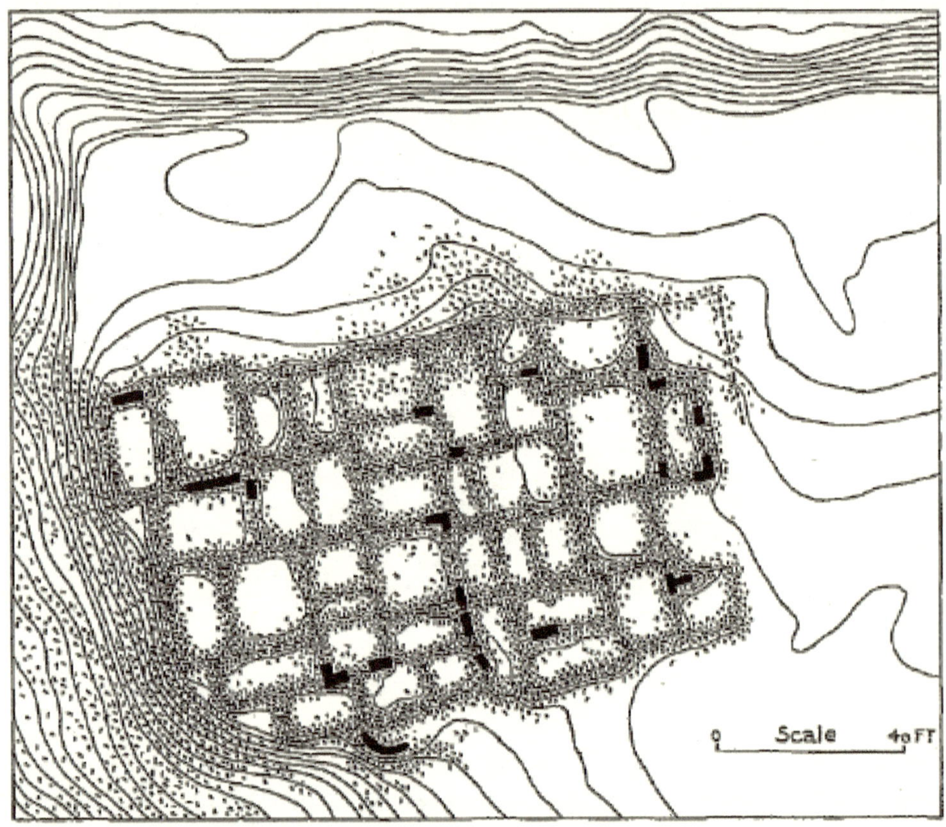

FIG. 280.—GROUND PLAN OF RUIN AT MOUTH OF THE EAST VERDE.

On the southern side of the East Verde, half a mile above its mouth, a small creek comes in from the south, probably dry throughout most of the year; and on a promontory or point of land left by this creek a small ruin occurs. It is similar in plan and in character of masonry to those just described, and differs from them only in that its site is better adapted for defense, being protected on two sides by steep hills or cliffs. The ground plan of this ruin is shown in figure 280, and its general appearance in plate XIV, which also shows the character of masonry. The village overlooked a large area of low bottom land in the angle between the Verde and the East Verde, and is itself overlooked by the foothills rising behind it to the high mesas forming part of the Mazatzal mountains.

PLATE XIV. RUIN AT MOUTH OF THE EAST VERDE.

The walls of this village were built of flat bowlders and slabs of limestone, and there is now practically no standing wall remaining. The ground plan shows a number of places where the walls are still visible, but they extend only a few inches above the debris. There were about forty rooms, and the plan is characterized by irregularities such as have already been noticed in other plans. Although the village was of considerable size it was built up solidly, and there is no trace of an interior court. It will be noticed that the rooms vary much in size, and that many of the smaller rooms are one half the size of the larger ones, as though the larger rooms had been divided by partitions after they were completed. It is probable that rooms extended partly down the slope on the west and south of the village toward the little creek before mentioned, but if this were the case all evidences have long since been obliterated.

On the southern side of the village the ground plan shows a bit of curved wall. It is doubtful whether this was an actual wall or merely a terrace. If it was a wall it is the only example of curved wall found in the region in ruins of this class. Between this wall or terrace and the adjoining wall on the north, with which it was connected, the ground is now filled in. Whether this filling occurred prior or subsequent to the abandonment of the village does not appear. The northeastern corner of the ruin is marked by a somewhat similar feature. Here there is a line of wall now almost obliterated and but feebly marked by debris, and the space between it and the village proper is partly filled in, forming a low terrace. Analogous features are found in several other ruins in this region, notably in the large ruin near Limestone creek. It should be noted in this connection that Mr. E. W. Nelson has found that places somewhat similar to these in the ruins about Springerville,

New Mexico, always well repaid the labor of excavation, and he adopted as a working hypothesis the assumption that these were the burial places of the village. Whether a similar condition would be found in this region can only be determined by careful and systematic excavation.

PLATE XV. MAIN COURT, RUIN AT MOUTH OF THE EAST VERDE.

The village did not occupy the whole of the mesa point on which it is located; on the east the ground rises gently to the foothills of the Mazatzal range, and on the south and west it slopes sharply down to the little creek before mentioned; while on the north there is a terrace or flat open space some 60 feet wide and almost parallel with the longer axis of the village. This open space and the sharp fall which limits it on the north is shown on the ground plan. The general view of the same feature (plate XV) also shows the character of the valley of the East Verde above the ruin; the stream is here confined within a low walled canyon. This open space formed a part of the village and doubtless occupied the same relation to it that interior courts do to other villages. Its northern or outer edge is a trifle higher than the space between it and the village proper and is marked by several large bowlders and a small amount of debris. It is possible that at one time there was a defensive wall here, although the ground falls so suddenly that it is almost impossible to climb up to the edge from below without artificial aid. Defensive walls such as this may have been are very rare in pueblo architecture, only one instance having been encountered by the writer in an experience of many years. The map seems to show more local relief to this terrace than the general view indicates, but it should be borne in mind that the contour interval is but 2½ feet.

PLATE XVI. RUIN AT MOUTH OF FOSSIL CREEK.

A comparison of the ground plan of this ruin and those previously described, together with that of the ruin near the mouth of Fossil creek (plate XVI), which is typical of this group, shows marked irregularity in outline and plan. In the character of the debris also this ruin differs from the Fossil creek ruin and others located near it. As in the latter, bowlders were used in the wall, but unlike the latter rough stone predominates. In the character of its masonry this ruin forms an intermediate or connecting link between the ruins near Limestone creek and opposite Verde and the class of which the ruin near the mouth of Fossil creek is typical. In the character of its site it is of the same class as the Fossil creek ruin, being intermediate between the valley pueblos, such as that near Limestone creek, and pueblos located on defensive sites, such as the group opposite Verde. The ground plan indicates an occupancy extending over a considerable period of time and terminating at or near the close of the period of aboriginal occupancy of the valley of Rio Verde.

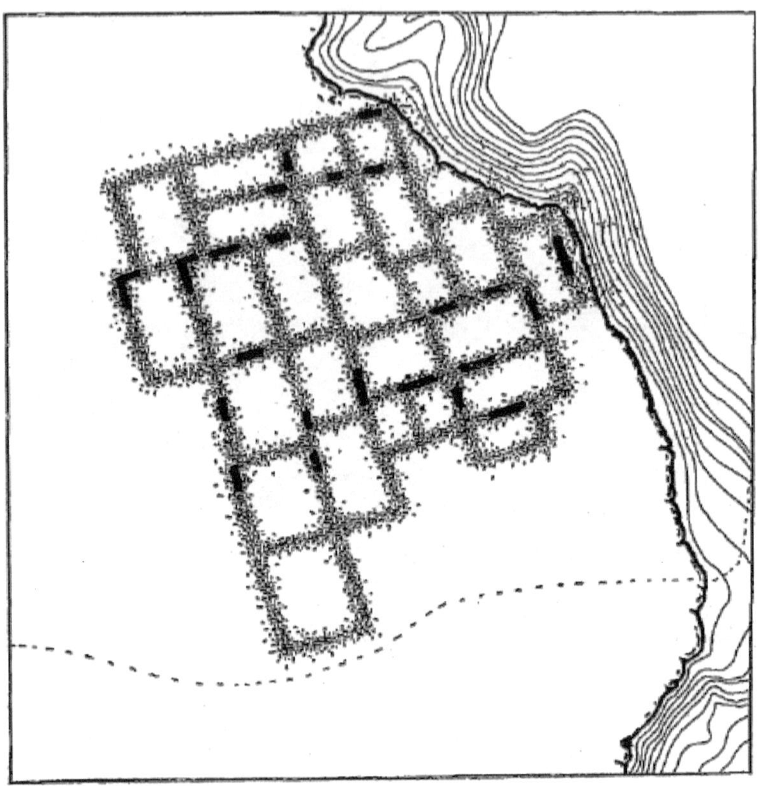

FIG. 281.—GROUND PLAN OF RUIN NEAR THE MONTH OF FOSSIL
CREEK.

Another ruin, of a type closely similar, occurs on a bluff near the mouth of Fossil creek. The plan of this ruin is shown in figure 281. The village is located close to the edge of the bluff, as shown in the plan, and has an outlook over a considerable area of bottom land adjoining the bluff on the east. It is probable that the cavate lodges whose location some 8 or 10 miles above the ruin, on Fossil creek, is shown on the general map (plate XI) were appendages of this village.

The wall still standing extends but a few inches above the débris, but enough remains to mark the principal wall lines, and these are farther emphasized by the lines of débris. The débris here is remarkably clean and stands out prominently from the ground surface, instead of being merged into it as is usually the case. This is shown in the general view of the ruin. There are twenty-five rooms on the ground plan, and there is no evidence that any of these attained a greater height than one story. The population, therefore, could not have been much, if any, in excess of forty, and as the average family of the Pueblos consists of five persons, this would make the number of families which found a home in this village less than ten. Notwithstanding this small population the ground plan of this village shows clearly a somewhat extended period of occupancy and a gradual growth in size. The eastern half of the village, which is located along the edge of the bluff, probably preceded the western in point of time. It will be noticed that while the wall lines are seldom continuous for more than three rooms, yet the rooms themselves are arranged with a certain degree of regularity, in that the longer axes are usually parallel.

The masonry of this village is almost entirely of flat bowlders, obtained probably from the bed of the creek immediately below. The terrace on which the village was built, and in fact all the hills about it are composed of gravel and bowlders, but it would be easier to carry the bowlders up from the stream bed than to quarry them from the hillside, and in the former case there would be a better opportunity for selection. Plate XVI shows the character of the rock employed, and illustrates the extent to which selection of rock has been carried. Although the walls are built entirely of river bowlders the masonry presents almost as good a face as some of the ruins previously described as built of slabs of limestone, and this is due to careful selection of the stone employed.

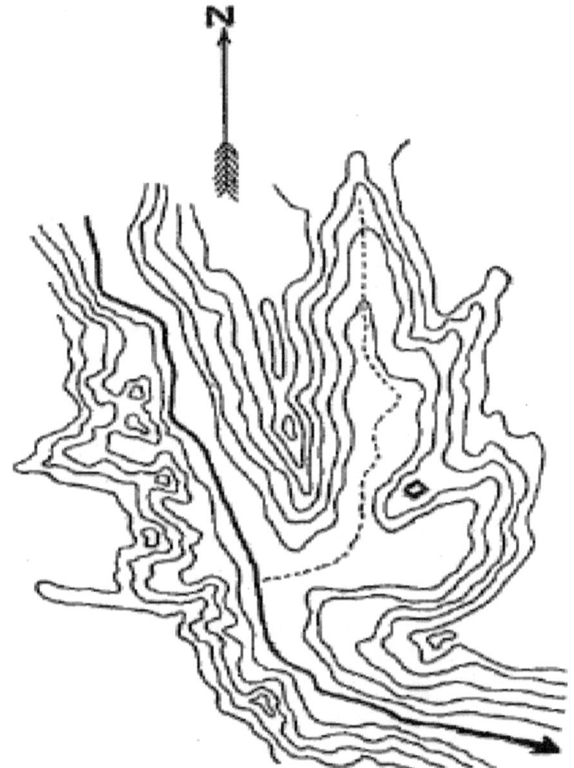

FIG. 282.—SKETCH MAP, SITE OF RUIN ABOVE FOSSIL CREEK.

About half a mile above the mouth of Fossil creek, and on the eastern side of the river, a deep ravine comes in from the north and east, and on a low spur near its mouth there is a ruin very similar to the one just described. It is also about the same size. The general character of the site it occupies is shown in the sketch, figure 282. The masonry is of the same general character as that of the ruin near the mouth of Fossil creek, and the débris, which stands out sharply from the ground surface, is distinguished by the same cleanness.

About 8½ miles north of Fossil creek, on the eastern side of the Verde, occurs a small ruin, somewhat different in the arrangement of rooms from those described. Here there is a bench or terrace, some 50 feet above the river, cut through near its northern end by a small canyon. The ruin is located on the southern side of this terrace, near the mouth of the creek, and consists of about ten rooms arranged in L shape. The lines are very irregular, and there are seldom more than three rooms connected. The débris marking the wall lines is clean, and the lines are well defined, although no standing wall remains.

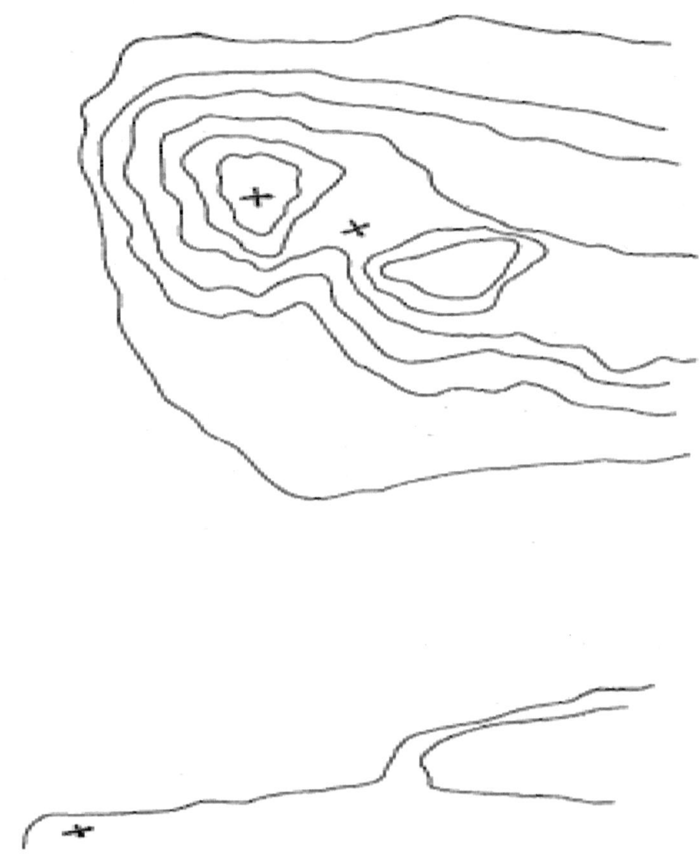

FIG. 283.—SKETCH MAP OF RUIN 9½ MILES ABOVE FOSSIL CREEK.

About a mile above the last-described ruin, or 9½ miles north of the mouth of Fossil creek, a small group of ruins occurs. The sketch, figure 283, shows the relation of the parts of this group to one another. The small cluster or rooms on the south is very similar in character, location, and size to the ruin last described. The northern portion is situated on the opposite side of a deep canyon or ravine, on the crown of a hill composed of limestone, which outcrops everywhere about it, and is considerably higher than the small cluster on the south. The northern ruin is of considerable size and very compactly built, the rooms being clustered about the summit of the hill. The central room, occupying the crown of the hill, is 20 feet higher than the outside rooms. In a saddle between the main cluster and a similar hill toward the southeast there are a number of other rooms, not marked so prominently by débris as those of the main cluster. There is no standing wall remaining, but the débris of the main and adjoining clusters indicates that the masonry was very rough, the walls being composed of slabs of limestone similar to those found in the large ruin near the mouth of Limestone creek, and obtained probably not 20 feet away from their present position.

The ruin described on page 200 and assigned to the first subclass occurs about half a mile north of this limestone hill, on the opposite side of the river. This small ruin, like all the smaller ruins described, was built of river bowlders, or river bowlders with occasional slabs of sandstone or limestone, while the ruin last described consists exclusively of limestone slabs. This difference is explained, however, by the character of the sites occupied by the several ruins. The limestone hill upon which the ruin under discussion is situated is an anomalous feature, and its occurrence here undoubtedly determined the location of this village. It is difficult otherwise to understand the location of this cluster of rooms, for they command no outlook over tillable land, although the view up and down the river is extensive. This cluster, which is the largest in size for many miles up and down the river, may have been the parent pueblo, occupying somewhat the same relation to the smaller villages that Zuñi occupies to the summer farming settlements of Nutria, Pescado, and Ojo Caliente; and doubtless the single-room remains, which occur above and below the cluster on mesa benches and near tillable tracts, were connected with it. This ruin is an example of the second subclass, or villages located on defensive sites, which merges into ruins of the first subclass, or villages on bottom lands, through villages like that located at the mouth of the East Verde and at the mouth of Fossil creek.

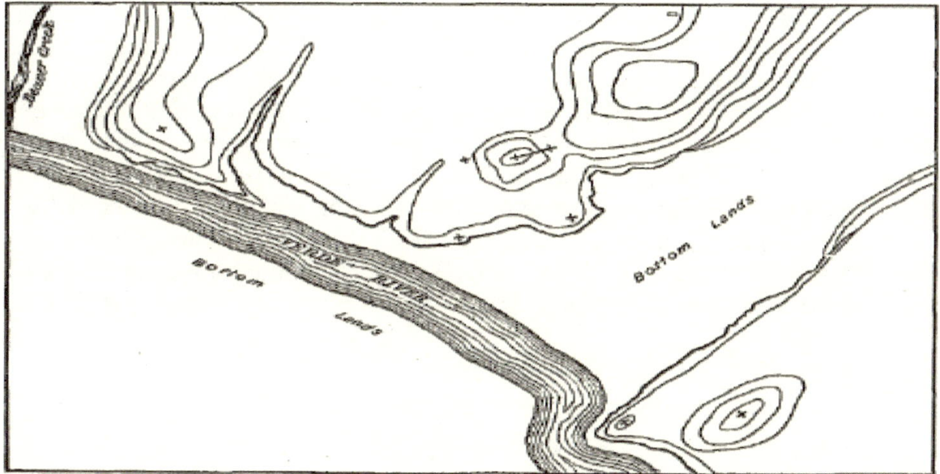

FIG. 284.—SKETCH MAP SHOWING LOCATION OF RUINS OPPO-
SITE VERDE.

On the eastern side of the Verde, just below the mouth of Beaver creek, opposite and a little above Verde, occurs one of the best examples to be found in this region of a large village located on a defensive site. Here there is a group of eight clusters extending half a mile up and down the river, and some of the clusters have walls still standing to a height of 8 and 10 feet. The relation of these clusters to each other is shown in the sketch map, figure 284.

PLATE XVII. GROUND PLAN OF RUINS OPPOSITE VERDE.

The principal ruin of the group is situated on the northern side of a small valley running eastward from the river up to the foot of a prominent mesa, which here bounds the eastern side of the river bottom. The valley is perhaps half a mile long and about an eighth of a mile wide. The ruin is located on a butte or knoll connected with the hills back of it by a low saddle, forming a sort of promontory or tongue of land rising from a flat space or bench, the whole some 200 feet above the river bottom. One of the clusters of rooms is located in the saddle mentioned and is connected with the main ruin. At the foot of the butte on the western side there is a similar cluster, not connected, however, with the main ruin; and south of the main ruin, on the extreme edge of the little mesa or bench, there is another small cluster. The ruin shown on the sketch map southwest of the main ruin consists of but two rooms, with no wall now standing. All these clusters are shown in their proper position on the ground plan, plate XVII. Plate XVIII, which is a general view from the east, shows the main ruin on the butte, together with the connected cluster east of it in the saddle. The modern settlement seen in the middle distance is Verde.

PLATE XVIII. GENERAL VIEW OF RUINS OPPOSITE VERDE.

About a quarter of a mile west of the main ruin there is another small but well-preserved cluster of rooms. It occupies the narrow ridge of a hill some 200 feet above the river. On the west and south, the hill descends abruptly to the river; on the southeast and east it slopes sharply down to a broad valley on the level of the mesa bench before mentioned, but the valley is cut by a narrow and deep canyon marking the east side of the hill. This cluster is shown on the ground plan, plate XVII, though not in its proper position. Northeast of this cluster and perhaps 200 yards distant there are traces of other rooms, but they are so faint that no plan can be made out. As shown on the sketch map, figure 284, the hill is a long narrow one, and its western side falls rapidly to a large triangular area of flat bottom land lying between it and Beaver creek, which it overlooks, as well as a large area of the valley up the river and all the fine bottom lands north and east of Verde and on the northwestern side of Beaver creek. As regards outlook, and also as regards security and facility of defense, the site of the small cluster is far superior to that of the main cluster of rooms.

PLATE XIX. SOUTHERN PART OF RUINS OPPOSITE VERDE.

About a quarter of a mile south and east of the main ruin, on the opposite side of the little valley before mentioned, a mesa bench similar to the one last described occurs; and on a point of this, extending almost to the river bank, there are traces, now nearly obliterated, of a small cluster of rooms. A short distance east of this point there is a large rounded knoll, with a peculiar terrace-like bench at about half its height. The entire summit of this knoll was occupied by rooms, of which the walls are much broken and none remain standing. This knoll, with the ruins on its summit, is shown in plate XIX, which also gives a general view from the north of the small cluster southeast of the main ruin. The character of the valley of the Verde at this point is also shown. The sketch map, figure 284, shows the location of these ruins in reference to others of the group.

The main cluster, that portion occupying the crown or summit of the butte before described, exhibits at the present time some fifty rooms in the ground plan, but there were at one time a larger number than this; and there is no doubt that rooms extended down the slopes of the hill southward and southwestward. The plan of this main cluster is peculiar; it differs from all the smaller surrounding clusters. It tells the story of a long occupancy by a people who increased largely in numbers, but who, owing to their hostile environment, could not increase the space occupied by them in proportion to their numbers. It will be noticed that while the wall lines are remarkably irregular in arrangement they are more often continuous than otherwise, more frequently continuous, in fact, than the lines of some of the smaller villages before described. The rooms are remarkably small, 10 feet square being a not unusual measurement, and built so closely together as to leave no space for interior courts. The typical rooms in the ruins of this region are oblong, generally about twice as long as broad, measuring approximately 20 by 10 feet.

In the ruin under discussion it seems that each of these oblong rooms was divided by a transverse partition into two smaller rooms, although the oblong form is also common. This is noticeable in the southwestern corner and on the eastern side of the main cluster, in the southwestern corner and on the northern end of the cluster adjoining on the north, and in all the smaller clusters. It is probable that the western central part of the main cluster was the first portion of the group of structures built, and that subsequently as the demand for accommodation increased, owing to increase of population, the rooms on the eastern and southern sides of the main cluster were added, while the rooms of the older portion were divided.

There is no evidence that any portion of this cluster attained a greater height than two stories, and only a small number of rooms reached that height. The small cluster adjoining on the north, and those on the southeast, southwest, and west, were built later and belong to the last period of the occupancy of the group. The builders exhibited a decided predilection for a flat site, as an examination of the sites of the various room clusters in the ground plan (plate XVII) will show, and when the sight of the main cluster became so crowded that additional rooms could be added only by building them on the sloping hillside, recourse was had to other sites. This tendency is also exhibited in the cluster adjoining the main cluster on the north, which was probably the second in point of age. The northern end of this small group of rooms terminates at the foot of the hill which rises northeastward, while a series of wall lines extends eastward at an angle with the lines of the cluster, but along the curve of the hillside.

The small northern cluster was in all probability inhabited by five or six families only, as contrasted with the main cluster, which had sixteen or seventeen, while the smaller clusters had each only two or three families. The strong presumption of the later building and occupancy of the smaller clusters, previously commented on, is supported by three other facts of importance, viz, the amount and height of the standing wall, the character of the sites occupied, and the extraordinary size of the rooms.

Although as a rule external appearance is an unsatisfactory criterion of age, still, other things equal, a large amount and good height of standing wall may be taken to indicate in a general way a more recent period of occupancy than wall lines much obliterated and merged into the surrounding ground level. The character of the site occupied is, however, a very good criterion of age. It was a rule of the ancient pueblo builder, a rule still adhered to with a certain degree of persistence, that enlargement of a village for the purpose of obtaining more space must be by the addition of rooms to those already built, and not by the construction of detached rooms. So well was this rule observed that attached rooms were often built on sites not at all adapted to them, when much better sites were available but a short distance away; and, although detached rooms were built in certain cases, there was always a strong reason for such exceptions to the general rule. At a late period in the history of the Pueblos this rule was not so much adhered to as before, and detached houses were often built at such points as the fancy or convenience of the builder might dictate. As the traditions are broken down the tendency to depart from the old rule becomes more decided, and at the present day several of the older Pueblo villages are being gradually abandoned for the more convenient detached dwellings, while nearly all of them have suffered more or less from this cause.

The tendency to cluster rooms in one large compact group was undoubtedly due primarily to hostile pressure from outside, and as this pressure decreased the inherent inconveniences of the plan would assert themselves and the rule would be less and less closely adhered to. It therefore follows that, in the absence of other sufficient cause, the presence of detached rooms or small clusters may be taken in a general way to indicate a more recent occupancy than a ground plan of a compact, closely built village.

The size of rooms is closely connected with the character of the site occupied. When, owing to hostile pressure, villages were built on sites difficult of access, and when the rooms were crowded together into clusters in order to produce an easily defended structure, the rooms themselves were necessarily small; but when hostile pressure from surrounding or outside tribes became less pronounced, the pueblo-builders consulted convenience more, and larger rooms were built. This has occurred in many of the pueblos and in the ruins, and in a general way a ruin consisting of large rooms is apt to be more modern than one consisting of small rooms; and where large and small rooms occur together there is a fair presumption that the occupancy of the village extended over a period when hostile pressure was pronounced and when it became less strong. It has already been shown that, owing to the social system of the pueblo-builders, there is almost always growth in a village, although the population may remain stationary in numbers or even decrease; so that, until a village is abandoned it will follow the general rule of development sketched above.

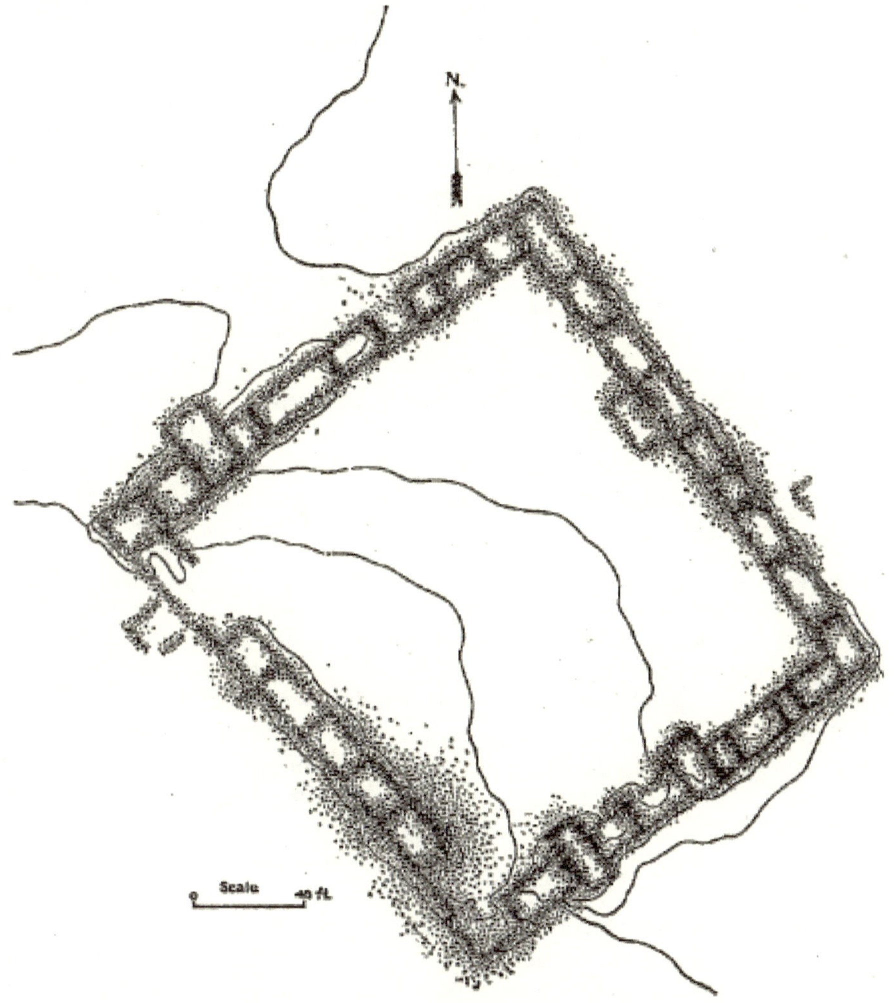

FIG. 285.—GROUND PLAN OF RUIN ON SOUTHERN SIDE OF
CLEAR CREEK.

Along the southern side of Clear creek, which discharges into the Rio Verde from the east, about 4 miles below Verde, there is a flat terrace from 30 to 40 feet above the creek and some 2 or 3 miles in length. Scattered over almost the whole of this terrace are remains of houses and horticultural works, which will be described later. Near the western end of the terrace a low hill with flat top and rounded sides rises, and on the top of this occurs the ruin whose ground plan is shown in figure 285.

This ruin commands an outlook over the whole extent of the terrace and seems to have been the home pueblo with which were connected the numerous single houses whose remains cover the terrace. The ground plan is peculiar. The rooms were arranged in four rows, each row consisting of a line of single rooms, and the rows were placed approximately at right angles to one another, forming the four sides of a hollow square. The rooms are generally oblong, of the usual dimensions, and as a rule placed with their longer axes in the direction of the row. Several rooms occur, however, with their longer axes placed across the row. Thirty-eight rooms can still be traced, and there is no likelihood that there were ever more than forty, or that any of the rooms attained a greater height than one story. The population, therefore, was probably never much in excess of fifty persons, or ten to twelve families.

It will be noticed that the wall lines are only approximately rectangular. The outside dimensions of the village are as follows: Northeastern side, 203 feet; southwestern, 207 feet; southeastern, 182 feet; and northwestern, 194 feet. The northeastern and southwestern sides are nearly equal in length, but between the southeastern and the northwestern sides there is a difference of 12 feet, and this notwithstanding that the room at the western end of the southeastern row has been set out 3 feet beyond the wall line of the southwestern side. This difference is remarkable if, as the ground plan indicates, the village or the greater part of it was laid out and built up at one time, and was not the result of slow growth.

As already stated, long occupancy of a village, even without increase of population, produces a certain effect on the ground plan. This effect, so strongly marked in all the ruins already described, is conspicuous in this ruin by its almost entire absence. The ground plan is just such as would be produced if a small band of pueblo builders, consisting of ten or twelve related families, should migrate en masse to a site like the one under discussion and, after occupying that site for a few years—less than five—should pass on to some other location. Such migration and abandonment of villages were by no means anomalous; on the contrary, they constitute one of the most marked and most persistent phenomena in the history of the pueblo builders. If the general principles, already laid down, affecting the development and growth of ground plans of villages are applied to this example, the hypothesis suggested above—an incoming of people en masse and a very short occupancy—must be accepted, for no other hypothesis will explain the regularity of wall lines, the uniformity in size of rooms, and the absence of attached rooms which do not follow the general plan of the village. The latter is perhaps the most remarkable feature in the ground plan of this village. The addition of rooms attached irregularly at various points of the main cluster, which is necessarily consequent on long occupancy of a site, even without increase of population, was in this example just commenced. The result of the same process, continued over a long period of time, can be seen in the ground plan of any of the inhabited villages of today and in most of the ruins, while a plan like that of the ruin under discussion, while not unknown, is rare.

PLATE XX. GENERAL VIEW OF RUIN ON SOUTHERN SIDE OF
CLEAR CREEK.

PLATE XXI. DETAILED VIEW OF RUIN ON SOUTHERN SIDE OF
CLEAR CREEK.

Plate XX, which is a general view of the ruin from the southwest, shows the
character of the site and the general appearance of the debris, while plate XXI illustrates the character of the masonry. It will be noticed that the level of the ground
inside and outside of the row of rooms is essentially the same; in other words,
there has been no filling in. It will also be noticed that the amount of debris is

small, and that it consists principally of rounded river bowlders. The masonry was peculiar, the walls were comparatively thin, and the lower courses were composed of river bowlders, not dressed or otherwise treated, while the upper courses, and presumably also the coping stones, were composed of slabs of sandstone and of a very friable limestone. The latter has disintegrated very much under atmospheric influences. The white areas seen in the illustrations are composed of this disintegrated limestone. The general appearance of the ruin at the present time must not be accepted as its normal condition. It is probable that the débris has undergone a process of artificial selection, the flat slabs and most available stones for building probably having been removed by neighboring settlers and employed in the construction of stone fences, which are much used in this region. Even with a fair allowance for such removal, however, there is no evidence that the rooms were higher than one story. The quantity of potsherds scattered about the ruins is noticeably small.

PLATE XXII. GENERAL VIEW OF RUIN 8 MILES NORTH OF FOSSIL CREEK.

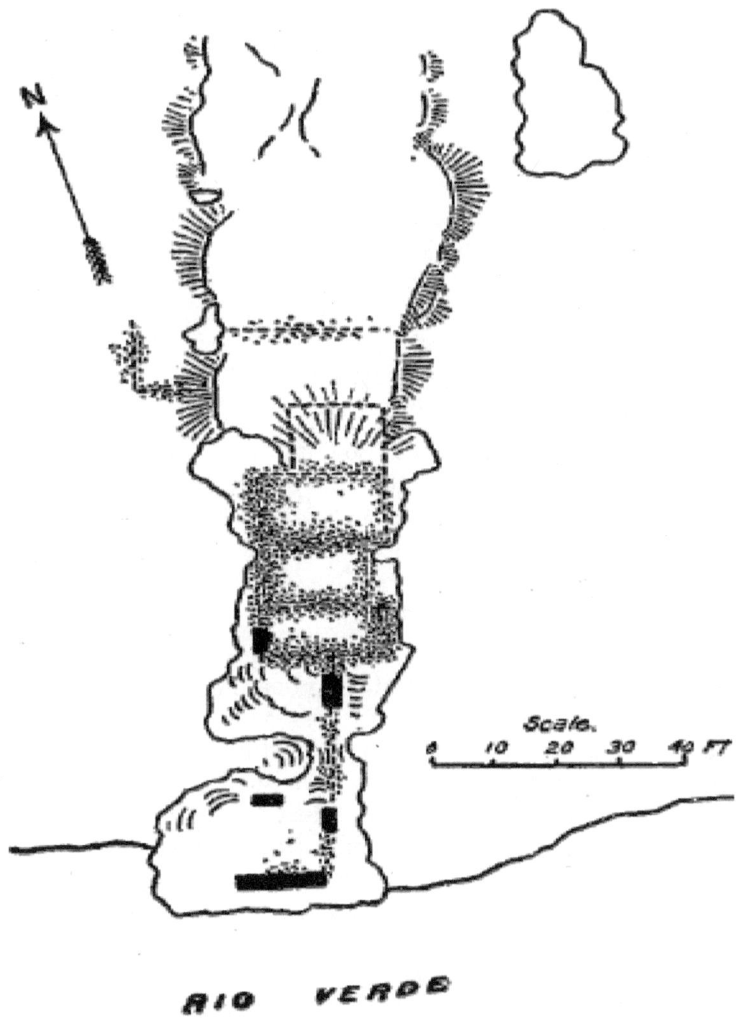

FIG. 286.—GROUND PLAN OF RUIN 8 MILES NORTH OF FOSSIL
CREEK.

About 8 miles north of the mouth of Fossil creek, on the eastern side of the
Verde, there is a ruin which, though very small, is interesting. At this point there is
a long narrow mass of rock, the remains of a volcanic dike, some 80 or 90 feet long,
which at the southern end overhangs the stream, while the other end is merged
into the ground level. At its southern end the rock is some 50 feet above the water,
but 150 feet northward the dike is no longer traceable. A general view of this dike
is given in plate XXII, while the ground plan, figure 286, shows the character of the
site. There were rooms on all that portion of the dike that stands out prominently
from the ground level, and traces of other rooms can be seen on the ground level
adjoining on the north and in the causeway resulting from the breaking down
and disintegration of the dike. Remains of eight rooms in all can be traced, five of

which were on the summit of the rock. The wall lines on the summit are still quite distinct and in places fragments of the original walls remain, as shown on the ground plan. The plan shows typical pueblo rooms of average size, and the masonry, though rough, is of the same character as that of other ruins in the vicinity.

Facility of defense undoubtedly had something to do with the choice of this location, but that it was not the only desideratum consulted is evident from the occurrence of a large area of fertile bottom land or flat river terrace immediately adjoining the ruin on the east and overlooked by it; in fact, the volcanic dike on which the ruin occurs occupies the western end of a large semicircular area of tillable land, such as already described. Viewed, however, as a village located with reference to defense it is the most perfect example—facility of obtaining water being considered—in this region. It may be used, therefore, to illustrate an important principle governing the location of villages of this type.

A study of the ground plan (figure 286) and the general view (plate XXII) will readily show that while the site and character of this village are admirably adapted for defense, so well adapted, in fact, as to suggest that we have here a fortress or purely defensive structure, still this adaptation arises solely from the selection of a site fitted by nature for the purpose, or, in other words, from an accident of environment. There has not been the slightest artificial addition to the natural advantages of the site.

The statement may seem broad, but it is none the less true, that, so far as our knowledge extends at the present time, fortresses or other purely defensive structures form a type which is entirely unknown in the pueblo region. The reason is simple; military art, as a distinct art, was developed in a stage of culture higher than that attained by the ancient pueblo builders. It is true that within the limits of the pueblo region structures are found which, from their character and the character of their sites, have been loosely described as fortresses, their describers losing sight of the fact that the adaptability of these structures to defense is the result of nature and not of art. Numerous examples are found where the building of a single short wall would double the defensive value of a site, but in the experience of the writer the ancient builders have seldom made even that slight addition to the natural advantages of the site they occupied.

The first desideratum in the minds of the old pueblo builders in choosing the location of their habitations was nearness to some area of tillable land. This land was generally adjacent to the site of the village, and was almost invariably overlooked by it. In fact this requirement was considered of far more importance than adaptability to defense, for the latter was often sacrificed to the former. A good example in which both requirements have been fully met is the ruin under discussion. This, however, is the result of an exceptionally favorable environment; as a rule the two requirements conflict with each other, and it is always the latter requirement—adaptability to defense—which suffers. These statements are true even of the so-called fortresses, of the cavate lodges, of the cliff ruins, and of many of the large village ruins scattered over the southwestern portion of the United States. In the case of the large village ruins, however, there is another feature of pueblo life which sometimes produces a different result, viz, the use of outlying single houses or small clusters separated from the main village and used for temporary abode during the farming season only. This feature is well developed in some of the modern pueblos, particularly in Zuñi and Acoma.

The principle illustrated by this ruin is an important one. Among the ancient pueblo builders there was no military art, or rather the military art was in its infancy; purely defensive structures, such as fortresses, were unknown, and the idea of defense never reached any greater development than the selection of an easily defended site for a village, and seldom extended to the artificial improvement of the site. There is another result of this lack of military knowledge not heretofore alluded to, which will be discussed at length on some other occasion and can only be mentioned here: this is the aggregation of a number of small villages or clusters into the large many-storied pueblo building, such as the modern Zuñi or Taos.

PLATE XXIII. GENERAL VIEW OF RUINS ON AN EMINENCE 14 MILES NORTH OF FOSSIL CREEK.

About 14 miles north of the mouth of Fossil creek, on the eastern side of the river, there is another ruin somewhat resembling the last described. A large red rock rises at the intersection of two washes, about a mile back from the river, and on a bench near the summit are the remains of walls. These are illustrated in plate XXIII. In general appearance and in character of site this ruin strongly resembles a type found in the San Juan region. There seem to have been only a few rooms on the top of the rock, and the prominent wall seen in the illustration was probably a retaining or filling wall in a cleft of the rock. Such walls are now used among the Pueblos for the sides of trails, etc. It is probable that at one time there were a considerable number of rooms on the rock; the debris on the ground at the base of the rock on the western side, shown in the illustration, is rather scanty; on the opposite or eastern side there is more, and it is not improbable there were rooms on the ground here. It is likely that access was from this side.

It should be noted that this ruin, which is of a type known as "fortress" by some writers, is so placed as to command an extensive outlook over the large valley below and over the two small valleys above, as well as the considerable area of flat or bottom land formed by the junction of the small valleys. It is a type of a subordinate agricultural settlement, and had the defensive motive been entirely absent from the minds of the builders of this village it would undoubtedly have been located just where it now is, as this is the best site for an agricultural settlement for some distance up and down the river.

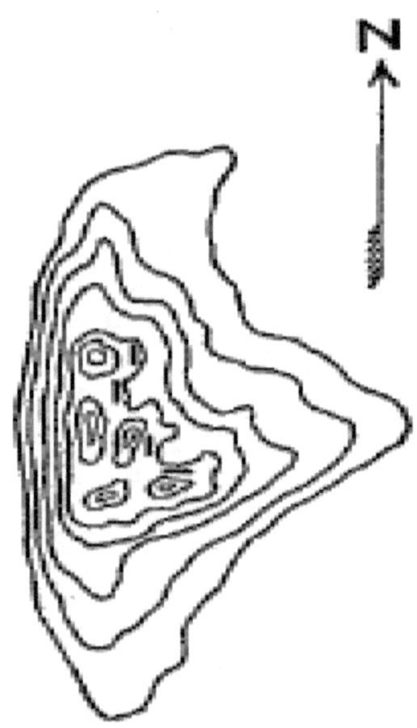

FIG. 287.—SKETCH MAP OF RUINS ON PINNACLE 7 MILES NORTH OF FOSSIL CREEK.

REMAINS OF walls somewhat similar to these last described occur on a butte or pinnacle on the eastern side of the river and about 7 miles north of the mouth of Fossil creek. From the south this pinnacle is a most conspicuous landmark, rising as it does some 2,500 feet above the river within a distance of a quarter of a mile. The upper 50 feet of the eminence consists of bare red rock split into sharp points and little pinnacles, as shown in figure 287, which represents only the upper portion of the butte. The heavy black lines on the sketch map are walls. Some of these were doubtless mere retaining walls, but others are still standing to a considerable height, and there is yet much débris on the slope of the rock forming the eastern side of the butte near its top. It is doubtful whether these rooms were ever used for habitations, and more probable that they were used as a shrine or for some analogous purpose.

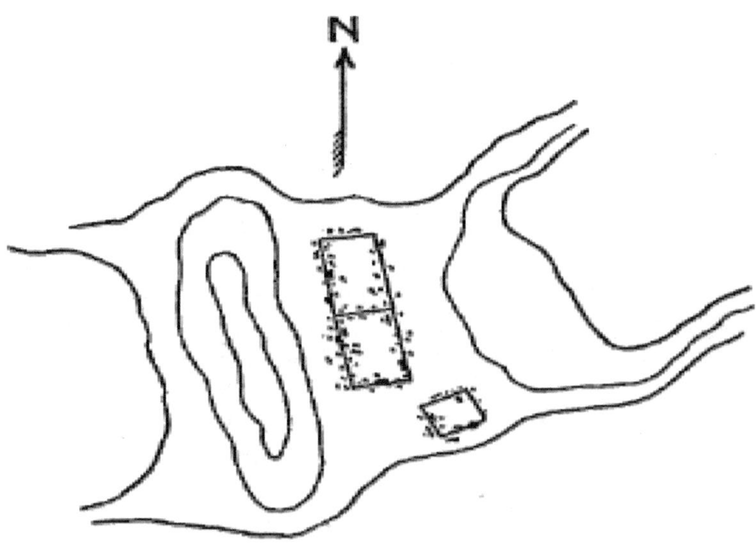

FIG. 288.—REMAINS OF SMALL ROOMS 7 MILES NORTH OF FOSSIL CREEK.

Perhaps a quarter of a mile northeastward, in the saddle connecting the butte with the contiguous hills in that direction, there are remains of three small rooms, located east of a low swell or ridge. Figure 288 shows the general character of the site, which seems to have been a favorite type for temporary structures, single-room outlooks, etc. Among the fragments of pottery picked up here were pieces of polished red ware of the southern type, and part of the bottom of a large pot of so-called corrugated ware.

Half a mile northwestward, in a saddle similar to that last described, and east of the crown of a hill, are the remains of a single room, nearly square and perhaps 10 feet long. These single rooms and small cluster remains are unusual in this region, and seem to replace the bowlder-marked ruins so common south of the East Verde (to be described more fully later). Although the walls of this single-room structure were built of river bowlders, they are well marked by débris and are of the same type as those in the ruins at the mouths of the East Verde and Fossil creek.

CAVATE LODGES.

Cavate lodges comprise a type of structures closely related to cliff houses and cave dwellings. The term is a comparatively new one, and the structures themselves are not widely known. They differ from the cliff houses and cave dwellings principally in the fact that the rooms are hollowed out of cliffs and hills by human agency, being cut out of soft rock, while the former habitations are simple, ordinary structures built for various reasons within a cove or on a bench in the cliffs or within a cave. The difference is principally if not wholly the result of a different physical environment, i.e., cavate lodges and cave dwellings are only different phases of the same thing; but for the present at least the name will be used and the cavate lodges will be treated as a separate class.

There are but three regions in the United States in which cavate lodges are known to occur in considerable numbers, viz, on San Juan river, near its mouth; on the western side of the Rio Grande near the pueblo of Santa Clara; and on the eastern slope of San Francisco mountain, near Flagstaff, Arizona. To these may now be added the middle Verde region, from the East Verde to a point north of Verde, Arizona.

Within the middle Verde region there are thousands of cavate lodges, sometimes in clusters of two or three, oftener in small groups, and sometimes in large groups comprising several hundred rooms. One of these large groups, located some 8 miles south of Verde on the eastern side of the river, has been selected for illustration.

PLATE XXIV. GENERAL VIEW OF NORTHERN END OF A GROUP
OF CAVATE LODGES.

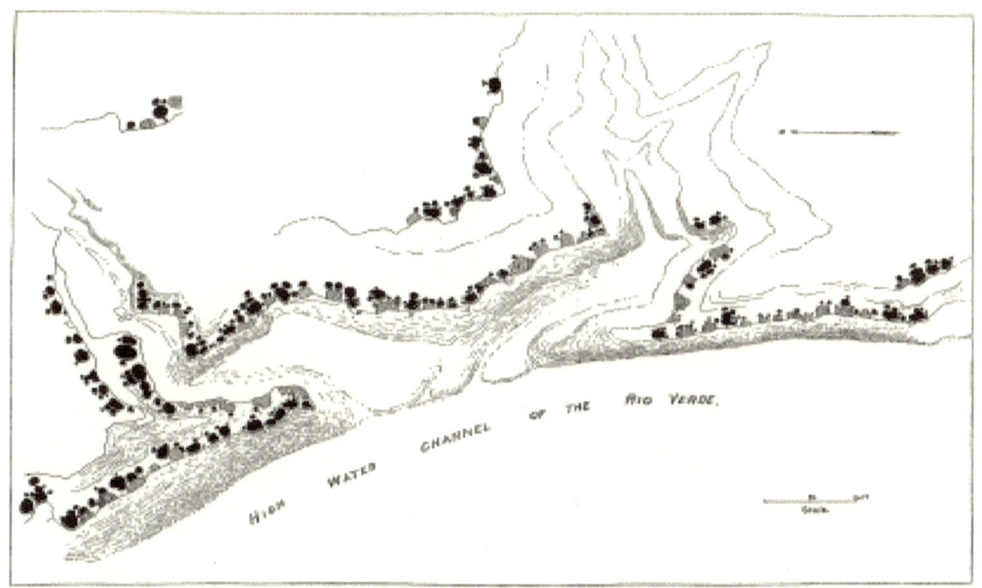

PLATE XXV. MAP OF GROUP OF CAVATE LODGES

The bottom lands of the Rio Verde in the vicinity of Verde have been already
described, and the cavate lodges in question occur just below the southern end of

this large area of tillable land, and some of them overlook it. The river at this point flows southward, and extending toward the east are two little canyons which meet on its bank. North and south of the mouth of the canyons the bank of the river is formed by an inaccessible bluff 180 or 200 feet high. These bluffs are washed by the Verde during high water, though there is evidence that up to a recent time there was a considerable area of bottom land between the river and the foot of the bluff. Plate XXIV shows the northern end of the group from a low mesa on the opposite side of the river; the eastern bank of the river can be seen in the foreground, while the sandy area extending to the foot of the bluff is the present high-water channel of the Verde. The map (plate XXV) shows the distribution of the cavate lodges composing the group, and plate XXVI shows the character of the site. The cavate lodges occur on two distinct levels—the first, which comprises nearly all the cavate lodges, is at the top of the slopes of talus and about 75 feet above the river; the second is set back from 80 to 150 feet from the first tier horizontally and 30 or 40 feet above it. The cavate lodges occur only in the face of the bluff along the river and in the lower parts of the two little canyons before mentioned. These canyons run back into the mesa seen in the illustration, which in turn forms part of the foothills rising into the range of mountains hemming in the Rio Verde on the east.

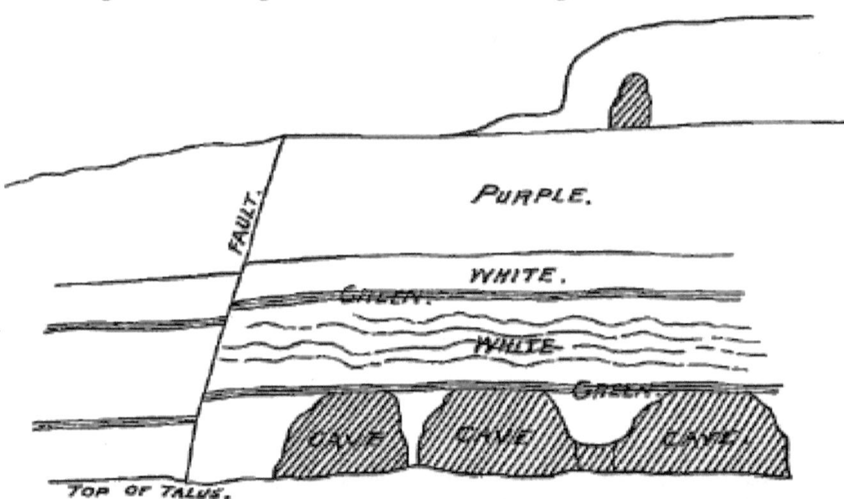

FIG. 289.—DIAGRAM SHOWING STRATA OF CANYON WALL.

The walls of the canyon in the cavate-lodge area are composed of three distinct strata, clearly defined and well marked. The relations of the strata, at points on the northern and western sides of the north canyon, are shown in figure 289 and plate XXVI. The lowest stratum shown in the figure is that in which almost all the cavate lodges occur. It is about 8 feet thick and composed of a soft, very friable, purple-gray sandstone. Above it lies a greenish-white bed a few inches thick, followed by a stratum of a pronounced white, about 12 feet thick. This heavy stratum is composed of calcareous clay, and the green bed of a calcareous clay with a mixture of sand. The white stratum is divided at two-thirds its height by a thin belt of greenish-white rock, and above it there is another belt of purple-gray sandstone about 12 feet thick. The top of this sandstone forms the ground surface south of the point shown in the diagram, while on the north and east it forms the floor of the upper tier of cavate lodges.

PLATE XXVI. STRATA OF NORTHERN CANYON WALL.

On the southern side of the canyon the lower purple stratum shows three distinct substrata; the upper is reddish purple and about 3½ feet thick, the middle is purple gray, about 7 feet thick, and apparently softer than the upper and lower strata. The lodges occur in the middle purple substratum, their floors composed of the upper surface of the lower stratum and their roofs of the under surface of the upper stratum. Those on the north side are similarly placed, their roofs being about 3 feet below the white, except that in several instances the upper part of the purple up to the white has fallen, making the cavity larger. This has occurred, however, since the abandonment of the caves, and the debris, still fresh looking, is in situ.

The formation in which the lodges occur is not of volcanic origin, although the beds composing it were perhaps deposited by hot springs during the period of great volcanic activity which produced San Francisco mountain in central Arizona and the great lava flows south of it. In view of the uncertainty on this point and the further fact that almost all the cavate lodges heretofore found were excavated in tufa, ash, or other soft volcanic deposits, the report of Mr. Joseph S. Diller, petrographer of the U.S. Geological Survey, will be of interest. It is as follows:

The coarse-grained specimen is sandstone, that of medium grain is argillaceous sandstone, and the fine-grained one is calcareous clay. The coarse-grained friable sandstone, in which the lodges have been excavated, consists chiefly of subangular and rounded grains of quartz and feldspar with a small proportion of black particles. Many of the latter are magnetite, while the others are hornblende and various ferromagnesian silicates. I did not detect any fragments of volcanic origin.

The specimen of argillaceous sandstone is made up of thin layers of fine-grained sand of the same sort as the first, alternating with others containing considerable clay. In the clay layers, a trace of carbonate of lime was found here and there, forming a transition of the calcareous clay.

The calcareous clay when placed in acid effervesces vigorously, but when allowed to stand the effervescence ceases in a few minutes and the insoluble white clay remains.

All the strata composing this formation are very soft; the purple-gray material of the middle layer is so soft that its surface can be rubbed off with the hand. They are also minutely stratified or laminated, and the laminæ are not well cemented together, so that a blow on the roof of a cavity with a stone or other implement will bring off slabs varying from half an inch to an inch and a half in thickness. These thin strata or laminæ are of unequal hardness, weathering in places several inches into the face of the rock in thin streaks of a few inches or less. The middle purple stratum exhibits this quality somewhat more decidedly than the others, and this fact has doubtless determined the selection of this stratum for the location of the lodges, as a room can be excavated in it more easily than a room of a similar size could be built up with loose rock.

The almost absolute dependence of the native builder on nature as he found it is well illustrated by these cavate lodges. At a point in the northern wall of the northernmost canyon, shown in the diagram (figure 289) and in plate XXVI, there is a small fault with a throw of about 2½ feet, and the floors of the lodges west of the fault are just that much lower than the floors east of it. Furthermore, where the purple-gray stratum in which the lodges occur is covered up by the rising ground surface, the cavate lodges abruptly cease. In the northern and southern ends of the group the talus encroaches on and partly covers the purple-gray stratum, and in these places the talus has been removed from the face of the rock to permit the excavation of lodges. In short, the occurrence of the cavate lodges in this locality is determined absolutely by the occurrence of one particular stratum, and when that stratum disappears the lodges disappear. So far as can be ascertained without actually excavating a room there is no apparent difference between the stratum in which the lodges occur and the other purple strata above and below it. That there is some difference is indicated by the confinement of the lodges to that particular level, but that the difference is very slight is shown by the occurrence in two places of lodges just above the principal tier, a kind of second-story lodge, as it were. It is such differences in environment as these, however, often so slight as to be readily overlooked, which determine some of the largest operations carried on by the native builders, even to the building of some of the great many-storied pueblos, and, stranger still, sometimes leading to their complete abandonment.

In the region under discussion cavate lodges usually occur in connection with and subordinate to village ruins, and range in number from two or three rooms to clusters of considerable size. Here, however, the cavate lodge is the feature which has been most developed, and it is noteworthy that the village ruins that occur in connection with them are small and unimportant and occupy a subordinate position.

PLATE XXVII. RUIN ON NORTHERN POINT OF CAVATE LODGE CANYON.

There are remains of two villages connected with the cavate lodges just described, perched on the points of the promontories which form the mouths of the two canyons before mentioned. The location of these ruins is shown in plate XXV. The one on the southern promontory is of greater extent than that on the northern point, and both are now much broken down, no standing wall remaining. A general view of the ruin on the northern promontory is given in plate XXVII, and the same illustration shows the remains of the other village on the flat top of the promontory in the farther part of the foreground. The cavate lodges are generally rudely circular in shape, sometimes oblong, but never rectangular. The largest are 25 and even 30 feet in diameter, and from this size range down to 5 or 6 feet and thence down to little cubby-holes or storage cists. Owing to their similarity, particularly in point of size, it is difficult to draw a line between small rooms and large storage cists, but including the latter there are two hundred rooms on the main level, divided into seventy-four distinct and separate sets. These sets comprise from one to fourteen rooms each. On the upper level there are fifty-six rooms, divided into twenty-four sets, making a total of two hundred and fifty-six rooms. As nearly as can be determined by the extent of these ruins the population of the settlement was probably between one hundred and fifty and two hundred persons.

There is great variety in the rooms, both in size and arrangement. As a rule each set or cluster of rooms consists of a large apartment, entered by a narrow passageway from the face of the bluff, and a number of smaller rooms connected with it by narrow doorways or short passages and having no outlet except through the large apartment. As a rule two or more of these smaller back rooms are attached to the main apartment, and sometimes the back rooms have still smaller rooms attached to them. In several cases there are three rooms in a series or row extending back into the rock, and in one instance (at the point marked E on the map, plate XXV) there are four such rooms, all of good size.

FIG. 290.—WALLED STORAGE CIST.

Attached to the main apartment, and sometimes also to the back rooms, there are usually a number of storage cists, differing from the smaller rooms of the cluster only in size. These cists or cubby-holes range in size from a foot to 5 feet in diameter, and are nearly always on a level of the floor, although in some instances they extend below it. Storage cists are also sometimes excavated in the exterior walls of the cliffs, and occasionally they are partly excavated and partly inclosed by a rough, semicircular wall. An example of the latter type is shown in figure 290.

PLATE XXVIII. CAVATE LODGE WITH WALLED FRONT.

As a rule the cavate lodges are set back slightly from the face of the bluff and connected with it by a narrow passageway. Another type, however, and one not uncommon, has no connecting passageway, but instead opens out to the air by a cove or nook in the bluff. This cove was used as the main room and the back rooms opened into it in the usual way by passageways. A number of lodges of this type can be seen in the eastern side of the northern promontory or bluff. Possibly lodges of this type were walled in front, although walled fronts are here exceptional, and some of them at least have been produced by the falling off of the rock above the doorway. The expedient of walling up the front of a shallow cavity, commonly practiced in the San Juan region, while comparatively rare in this vicinity, was known to the dwellers in these cavate lodges. At several points remains of front walls can be seen, and in two instances front walls remain in place. The masonry, however, is in all cases very rough, of the same type as that shown in plate XXVIII.

PLATE XXIX. OPEN FRONT CAVATE LODGES ON THE RIO SAN JUAN.

PLATE XXX. WALLED FRONT CAVATE LODGES ON THE RIO SAN JUAN.

In this connection a comparison with the cavate ledges found in other regions will be of interest. In 1875 Mr. W. H. Holmes, then connected with the Hayden survey, visited a number of cavate lodges on the Rio San Juan and some of its tributaries. Several groups are illustrated in his report.[5] Two of his illustrations, showing, respectively, the open front and walled front lodges, are reproduced in plates XXIX and XXX. The open front lodges are thus described:

[5] Tenth Ann Rep. U.S. Geol. Survey, 1876, pp. 288-391.

I observed, in approaching from above, that a ruined tower stood near the brink of the cliff, at a point where it curves outward toward the river, and in studying it with my glass detected a number of cave-like openings in the cliff face about halfway up. On examination, I found them to have been shaped by the hand of man, but so weathered out and changed by the slow process of atmospheric erosion that the evidences of art were almost obliterated.

The openings are arched irregularly above, and generally quite shallow, being governed very much in contour and depth by the quality of the rock. The work of excavation has not been an extremely great one, even with the imperfect implements that must have been used, as the shale is for the most part soft and friable.

A hard stratum served as a floor, and projecting in many places made a narrow platform by which the inhabitants were enabled to pass along from one house to another.

Small fragments of mortar still adhered to the firmer parts of the walls, from which it is inferred that they were at one time plastered. It is also extremely probable that they were walled up in front and furnished with doors and windows, yet no fragment of wall has been preserved. Indeed, so great has been the erosion that many of the caves have been almost obliterated, and are now not deep enough to give shelter to a bird or bat.

Walled fronts, the author states, were observed frequently on the Rio Mancos, where there are many well-preserved specimens. He described a large group situated on that stream, about 10 miles above its mouth, as follows:

The walls were in many places quite well preserved and new looking, while all about, high and low, were others in all stages of decay. In one place in particular, a picturesque outstanding promontory has been full of dwellings, literally honeycombed by this earth-burrowing race, and as one from below views the ragged, window-pierced crags [see plate XXX] he is unconsciously led to wonder if they are not the ruins of some ancient castle, behind whose moldering walls are hidden the dread secrets of a long-forgotten people; but a nearer approach quickly dispels such fancies, for the windows prove to be only the doorways to shallow and irregular apartments, hardly sufficiently commodious for a race of pigmies. Neither the outer openings nor the apertures that communicate between the caves are large enough to allow a person of large stature to pass, and one is led to suspect that these nests were not the dwellings proper of these people, but occasional resorts for women and children, and that the somewhat extensive ruins in the valley below were their ordinary dwelling places.

It will be noticed that in both these cases there are associated ruins on the mesa top above, and in both instances these associated ruins are subordinate to the cavate lodges, in this respect resembling the lodges on the Verde already described. This condition, however, is not the usual one; in the great majority of cases the cavate lodges are subordinate to the associated ruins, standing to them in the relation of outlying agricultural shelters. Unless this fact is constantly borne in mind it is easy to exaggerate the importance of the cavate lodges as compared with the village ruins with which they are connected.

The cavate lodges near San Francisco mountain in Arizona were visited in 1883 by Col. James Stevenson, of the Bureau of Ethnology, and in 1885 by Maj. J. W. Powell. Major Powell[6] describes a number of groups in the vicinity of Flagstaff. Of one group, situated on a cinder cone about 12 miles east of San Francisco peak, he says:

Here the cinders are soft and friable, and the cone is a prettily shaped dome. On the southern slope there are excavations into the indurated and coherent cinder mass, constituting chambers, often 10 or 12 feet in diameter and 6 to 10 feet in height. The chambers are of irregular shape, and occasionally a larger central chamber forms a kind of vestibule to several smaller ones gathered about it. The smaller chambers are sometimes at the same altitude as the central or principal one, and sometimes at a lower altitude. About one hundred and fifty of these chambers have been excavated. Most of them are now partly filled by the caving in of the walls and ceilings, but some of them are yet in a good state of preservation. In these chambers, and about them on the summit and sides of the cinder cone, many stone implements were found, especially metates. Some bone implements also were discovered. At the very summit of the little cone there is a plaza, inclosed by a rude wall made of volcanic cinders, the floor of which was carefully leveled. The plaza is about 45 by 75 feet in area. Here the people lived in underground houses—chambers hewn from the friable volcanic cinders. Before them, to the south, west, and north, stretched beautiful valleys, beyond which volcanic cones are seen rising amid pine forests. The people probably cultivated patches of ground in the low valleys.

About 18 miles still farther to the east of San Francisco mountain, another ruined village was discovered, built about the crater of a volcanic cone. This volcanic peak is of much greater magnitude. The crater opens to the eastward. On the south many stone dwellings have been built of the basaltic and cinder-like rooks. Between the ridge on the south and another on the northwest there is a low saddle in which other buildings have been erected, and in which a great plaza was found, much like the one previously described. But the most interesting part of this village was on the cliff which rose on the northwest side of the crater. In this cliff are many natural caves, and the caves themselves were utilized as dwellings by inclosing them in front with walls made of volcanic rocks and cinders. These cliff dwellings are placed tier above tier, in a very irregular way. In many cases natural caves were thus utilized; in other cases cavate chambers were made; that is, chambers have been excavated in the friable cinders. On the very summit of the ridge stone buildings were erected, so that this village was in part a cliff village, in part cavate, and in part the ordinary stone pueblo. The valley below, especially to the southward, was probably occupied by their gardens. In the chambers among the overhanging cliffs a great many interesting relics were found, of stone, bone, and wood, and many potsherds.

It will be seen that the first group described bears a remarkably close resemblance to the cavate lodges on the Rio Verde. The lodges themselves are smaller, but the arrangement of main apartment and attached back rooms is quite similar.

[6] Seventh Ann. Rep. Bur. Eth., 1891, p. xix.

It will be noticed also that in the second group described village ruins are again associated on the summit of the cliff or ridge. Major Powell ascertained that these cavate lodges were occupied by the Havasupai Indians now living in Cataract canyon, who are closely related to the Walapai, and who, it is said, were driven from this region by the Spaniards.

The cavate lodges on the Rio Grande, in New Mexico, in the vicinity of the modern pueblo of Santa Clara, were also visited in 1885 by Major Powell and are thus described by him:[7]

The cliffs themselves are built of volcanic sands and ashes, and many of the strata are exceedingly light and friable. The specific gravity of some of these rocks is so low that they will float on water. Into the faces of these cliffs, in the friable and easily worked rock, many chambers have been excavated; for mile after mile the cliffs are studded with them, so that altogether there are many thousands. Sometimes a chamber or series of chambers is entered from a terrace, but usually they were excavated many feet above any landing or terrace below, so that they could be reached only by ladders. In other places artificial terraces were built by constructing retaining walls and filling the interior next to the cliffs with loose rock and sand. Very often steps were cut into the face of a cliff and a rude stairway formed by which chambers could be reached. The chambers were very irregularly arranged and very irregular in size and structure. In many cases there is a central chamber, which seems to have been a general living room for the people, back of which two, three, or more chambers somewhat smaller are found. The chambers occupied by one family are sometimes connected with those occupied by another family, so that two or three or four sets of chambers have interior communication. Usually, however, the communication from one system of chambers to another was by the outside. Many of the chambers had evidently been occupied as dwellings. They still contained fireplaces and evidences of fire; there were little caverns or shelves in which various vessels were placed, and many evidences of the handicraft of the people were left in stone, bone, horn, and wood, and in the chambers and about the sides of the cliffs potsherds are abundant. On more careful survey it was found that many chambers had been used as stables for asses, goats, and sheep. Sometimes they had been filled a few inches, or even 2 or 3 feet, with the excrement of these animals. Ears of corn and corncobs were also found in many places. Some of the chambers were evidently constructed to be used as storehouses or caches for grain. Altogether it is very evident that the cliff houses have been used in comparatively modern times; at any rate, since the people owned asses, goats, and sheep. The rock is of such a friable nature that it will not stand atmospheric degradation very long, and there is abundant evidence of this character testifying to the recent occupancy of these cavate dwellings.

Above the cliffs, on the mesas, which have already been described, evidences of more ancient ruins were found. These were pueblos built of cut stone rudely dressed. Every mesa had at least one ancient pueblo up off it, evidently far more ancient than the cavate dwellings found in the face of the cliffs. It is, then, very plain that the cavate dwellings are not of great age; that they have been occupied

[7] Seventh Ann. Rep. Bur. Eth., op. cit., p. XXII.

since the advent of the white man, and that on the summit of the cliffs there are ruins of more ancient pueblos.

Major Powell obtained a tradition of the Santa Clara Indians, reciting three successive periods of occupancy of the cavate lodges by them, the last occurring after the Spanish conquest of New Mexico in the seventeenth century.

PLATE XXXI. CAVATE LODGES ON THE RIO GRANDE.

It will be noticed that here again the cavate lodges and village ruins are associated, although in this case the village ruins on the mesas above are said to be more ancient than the cavate lodges. A general view of a small section of cliff containing lodges is given in plate XXXI for comparison with those on the Verde. The lodges on the Rio Grande seem to have been more elaborate than those on the Verde, perhaps owing to longer occupancy; but the same arrangement of a main front room and attached back rooms, as in the cavate lodges on the Verde, was found.

As the cavate lodges of the San Francisco mountain region have been assigned to the Havasupai Indians of the Yuman stock, and those of the Rio Grande to the Santa Clara pueblo Indians of the Tanoan stock, it may be of interest to state that there is a vague tradition extant among the modern settlers of the Verde region that the cavate lodges of that region were occupied within the last three generations. This tradition was derived from an old Walapai Indian whose grandfather was alive when the cavate lodges were occupied. It was impossible to follow this tradition to its source, and it is introduced only as a suggestion. Attention is called, however, to the tradition given in the introduction to this paper with which it may be connected.

PLATE XXXII. INTERIOR VIEW OF CAVATE LODGE, GROUP D.

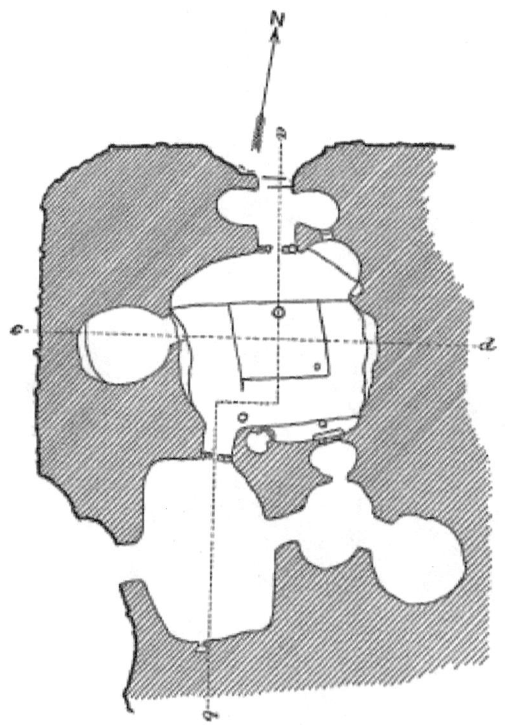

FIG. 291.—PLAN OF CAVATE LODGES, GROUP D.

Aside from the actual labor of excavation, there was but little work expended on the Verde cavate lodges. The interiors were never plastered, so far as the writer could determine. Figure 291 shows the plan of one of the principal sets of rooms, which occurs at the point marked D on the map, plate XXV; and plate XXXII is an interior view of the principal room, drawn from a flashlight photograph. This set of rooms was excavated in a point of the cliff and extends completely through it as shown on the general plan, plate XXV. The entrance was from the west by a short passageway opening into a cove extending back some 10 feet from the face of the cliff. The first room entered measures 16 feet in length by 10 feet in width. On the floor of this room a structure resembling the piki or paper bread oven of the Tusayan Indians, was found constructed partly of fragments of old and broken metates. At the southern end of the room there is a cubby-hole about a foot in diameter, excavated at the floor level. At the eastern end of the room there is a passageway about 2½ feet long leading into a smaller roughly circular room, measuring 7½ feet in its longest diameter, and this in turn is connected with another almost circular room of the same size. The floors of all three of these rooms are on the same level, but the roofs of the two smaller rooms are a foot lower than that of the entrance room. At the northern end of the entrance room there is a passageway 3 feet long and 2½ feet wide leading into the principal room of the set. This passageway at its southern end has a framed doorway of the type illustrated later.

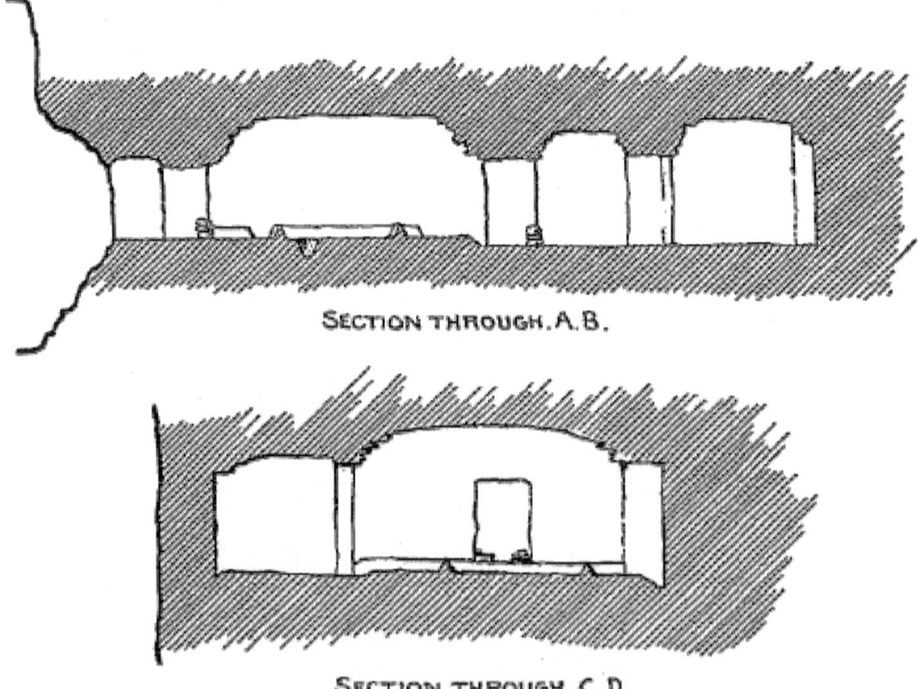

FIG. 292.—SECTIONS OF CAVATE LODGES, GROUP D.

The main room is roughly circular in form, measuring 16 feet in its north and south diameter and 15 feet from east to west. The roof is about 7 feet above the floor. Figure 292 shows a section from northwest to southwest (a, b, figure 291) through the small connected room adjoining on the south, and also an east arid west section (c, d, figure 291). The floor is plastered with clay wherever it was necessary in order to bring it to a level, and the coating is consequently not of uniform thickness. It is divided into sections by low ridges of clay as shown in the plan and sections; the northern section is a few inches higher than the other. Extending through the clay finish of the floor and into the rock beneath there are four pits, indicated on the plan by round spots. The largest of these, situated opposite the northern door, was a fire hole or pit about 18 inches in diameter at the floor level, of an inverted conical shape, about 10 inches in depth, and plastered inside with clay inlaid with fragments of pottery placed as closely together as their shape would permit. The other pits are smaller; one located near the southeastern corner of the room is about 6 inches in diameter and the same in depth, while the others are mere depressions in the floor, in shape like the small paint mortars used by the Pueblos.

The room, when opened, contained a deposit of bat dung and sand about 3 feet thick in the center and averaging about 2 feet thick throughout the room. This deposit exhibited a series of well-defined strata, varying from three-fourths to an inch and a half thick, caused by the respective predominance of dung or sand. No evidence of disturbance of these strata was found although careful examination was made. This deposit was cleared out and a number of small articles were found, all resting, however, directly on the floor. The articles consisted of fragments of basketry, bundles of fibers and pieces of fabrics, pieces of arrowshafts, fragments of grinding stones, three sandals of woven yucca fiber, two of them new and nearly perfect, and a number of pieces of cotton cloth, the latter scattered over the room and in several instances gummed to the floor. Only a few fragments of pottery were found in the main room, but outside in the northern passageway were the fragments of two large pieces, one an olla, the other a bowl, both buried in 3 or 4 inches of debris under a large slab fallen from the roof.

Owing to its situation this room was one of the most desirable in the whole group. The prevailing south wind blows through it at all times, and this is doubtless the reason that it was so much filled up with sand. In the center of the room the roof has fallen at a comparatively recent date from an area about 10 by 7 feet, in slabs about an inch thick, for the fragments were within 6 inches of the top of the debris. The walls are smoke-blackened to a very slight extent compared with the large room south of it.

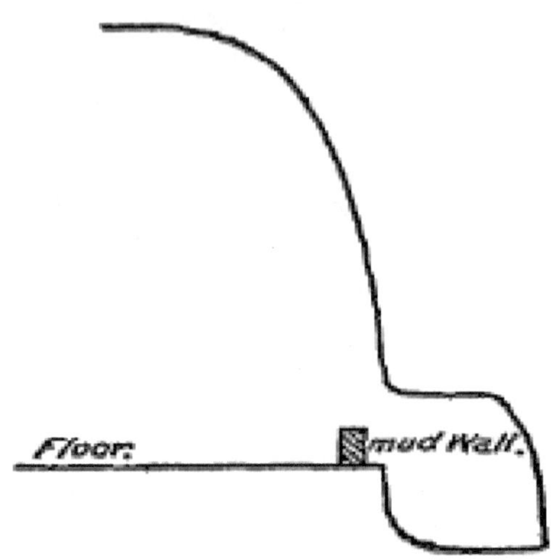

FIG. 293.—SECTION OF WATER POCKET.

At the northeastern and southwestern corners there are two small pockets, opening on the floor level but sunk below it, which seem to have been designed to contain water. That in the southwest corner is the larger; it is illustrated in the section, figure 293. As shown in the section and on the plan (figure 291), a low wall composed of adobe mortar and broken rock was built across the opening on the edge of the floor, perhaps to increase its capacity. This cavity would hold 15 to 20 gallons of water, a sufficient amount to supply the needs of an ordinary Indian family for three weeks or a mouth. The pocket in the northeastern corner of the room is not quite so large as the one described, and its front is not walled.

West of the main room there is a storage room, nearly circular in shape, with a diameter of about 6 feet and with a floor raised about 2 feet above that of the main room. Its roof is but 3 feet above the floor, and across its western end is a low bench a couple of inches above the floor. In the northeastern corner there is a shallow cove, also raised slightly above the main floor and connecting by a narrow opening with the outer vestibule-like rooms on the north. These northern rooms of the lodge seem to be simply enlargements of the passageway. The northern opening is a window rather than a door as it is about 10 feet above the ground and therefore could be entered only by a ladder. The opening is cut in the back of a cove in the cliff, and is 6 feet from the northern end of the main room. At half its length it has been enlarged on both sides by the excavation of niches or coves about 4 feet deep but only 2½ feet high. These coves could be used only for storage on a small scale.

In the southeastern corner of the main room there is another opening leading into a low-roofed storage cist, approximating 4 feet in diameter, and this cist was in turn connected with the middle one of the three rooms first described. This opening, at the time the room was examined, was so carefully sealed and plastered that it was scarcely perceptible.

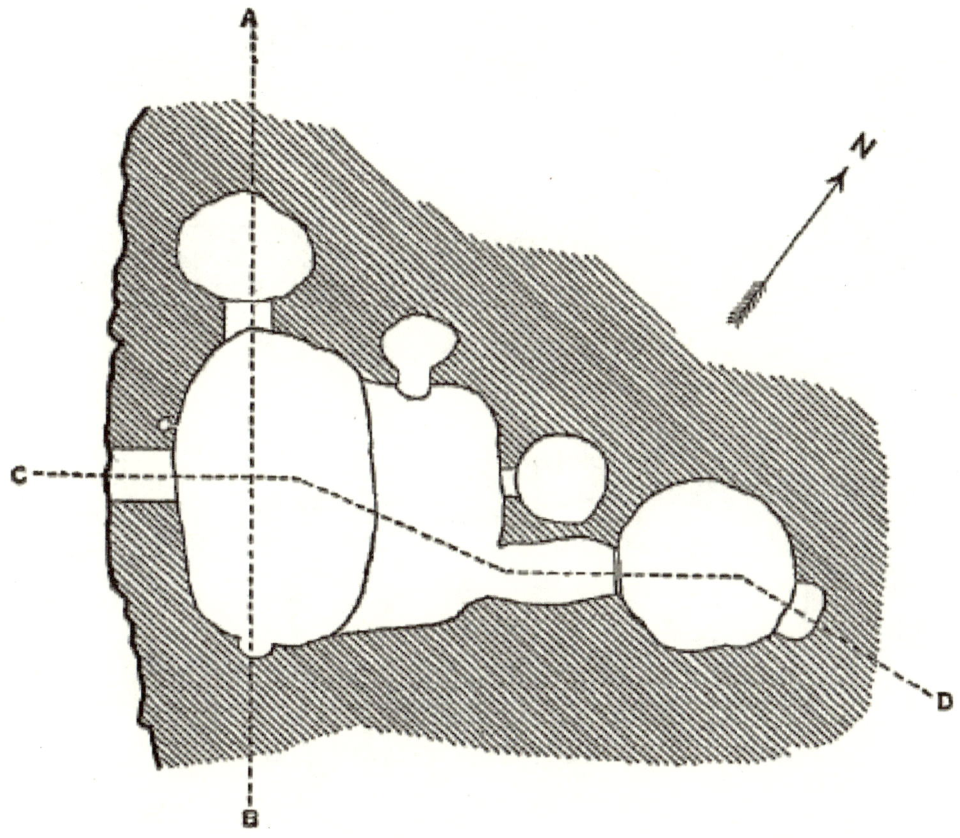

FIG. 294.—PLAN OF CAVATE LODGES, GROUP A.

A different arrangement of rooms is shown in plan in figure 294 and in section in figure 295. This group occurs at the point marked A on the map. The entrance to the main room was through a narrow passage, 3 feet long, leading into the chamber from the face of the bluff, which at this point is vertical. The main room is oblong, measuring 17 feet one way and 10 the other. At the southern end there is a small cist and on the western side near the entrance there is another hardly a foot in diameter. North of the main room there is a small, roughly circular room with a diameter of about 6 feet. It is connected with the main room by a passage about 2 feet long. On the floor of the main room there are two low ridges of clay, similar to those already described, which divide it into three sections of nearly equal size.

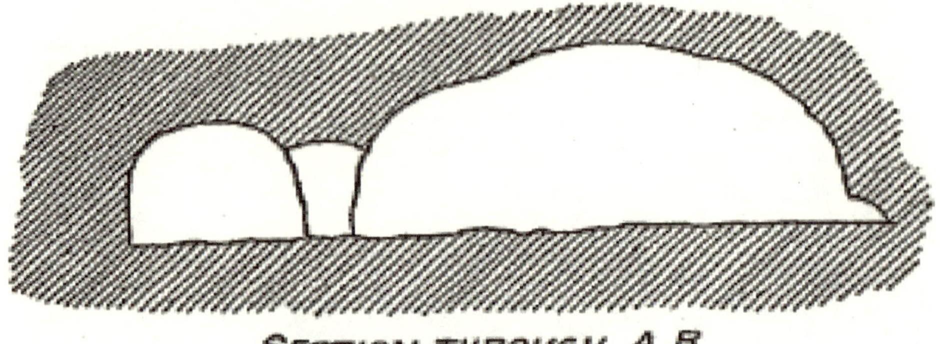

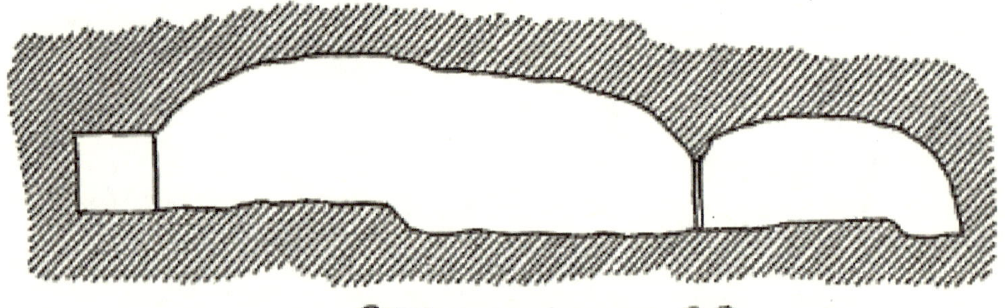

FIG. 295.—SECTIONS OF CAVATE LODGES, GROUP A.

East of the main room there is another of considerable size in the form of a bay or cove. It measures 13 feet by 6 feet, and its floor is 20 inches higher than that of the main room, as shown in the section (figure 295). Attached to this bay, at its northern end, is a small cist about 3 feet in diameter, and with its floor sunk to the level of the floor of the main room. East of the cove there is another cist about 4½ feet in diameter and with its floor on the level of the cove. Adjoining it on the south and leading out from the southeastern corner of the cove or bay, there is a long passage leading into an almost circular room 9 feet in diameter. The back wall of this room is 33 feet from the face of the cliff. The passage leading into it is 6 feet long, 2½ feet wide at the doorways, bulging slightly in the center, and its floor is on the same level as the rooms it connects; its eastern end is defined by a ridge of clay about 6 inches high.

In the eastern side of the circular room last described there is a storage cist about 3 feet wide and 2 feet deep. No fire-pit was seen in this cluster, although if the principal apartment were carefully cleaned out it is not improbable that one might be found.

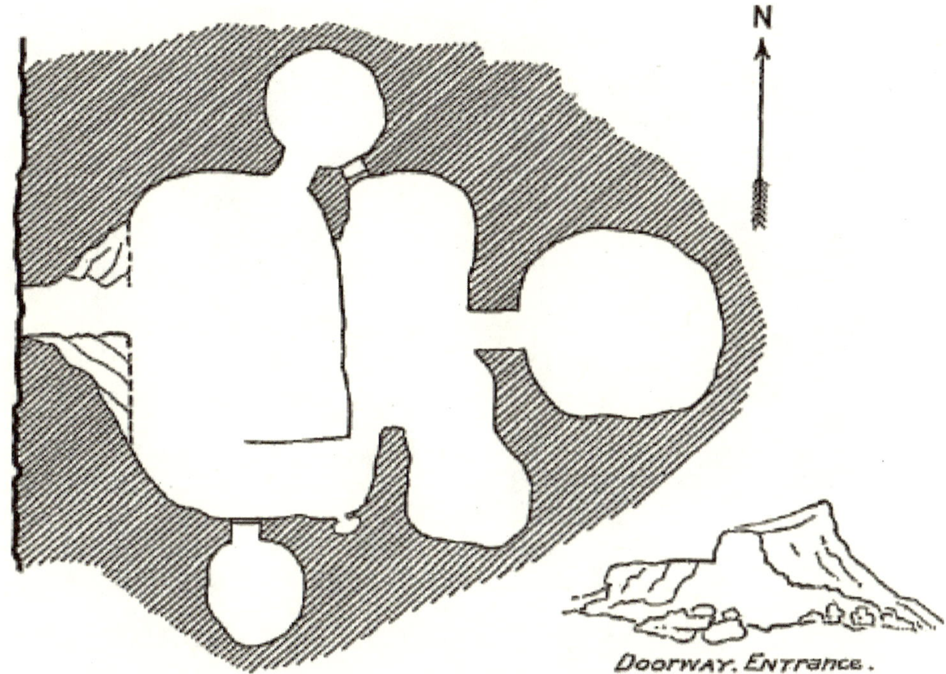

FIG. 296.—PLAN OF CAVATE LODGES, GROUP B.

A cluster of rooms somewhat resembling the last described is shown in plan in figure 296. This cluster occurs at the point marked *B* on the map. The main room is set back 5½ feet from the face of the bluff, which is vertical at this point, and is oblong in shape, measuring 19½ by 11½ feet. Its roof is 7½ feet above the floor in the center of the room. Attached to its southern end by a passage only a foot in length is a small room or storage cist about 5 feet in diameter. At its northeastern corner there is another room or cist similar in shape, about 7 feet in diameter, and reached by a passage 2 feet long. This small room is also connected with a long room east of the main apartment by a passage, the southern end of which was carefully sealed up and plastered, making a kind of niche of the northern end. At the southeastern corner of the room there is a small niche about 2 feet in diameter on the level of the floor.

The eastern side of the main room is not closed, but opens directly into an oblong chamber of irregular size with the roof nearly 2 feet lower and the floor a foot higher than the main room. This step in the floor is shown by the line between the rooms on the ground plan. The second room is about 6 feet wide and 20 feet long, its southern end rounding out slightly so as to form an almost circular chamber. Near the center of its eastern side there is a passageway 2½ feet long leading into a circular chamber 10½ feet in diameter and with its floor on the same level as the room to which it is attached. The back wall of this room is 35½ feet from the face of the cliff.

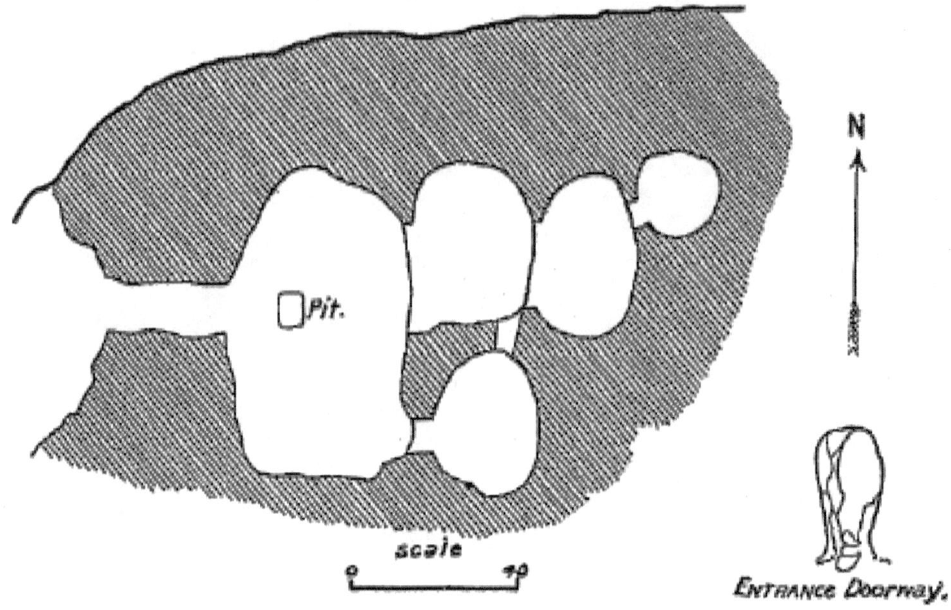

FIG. 297.—PLAN OF CAVATE LODGES, GROUP E.

A group occurring at the point marked E on the map (plate XXV) is shown in plan in figure 297. It is located in a projecting corner of the bluff and marks the eastern limit of the cavate lodges at this end of the canyon. The group consists of five rooms, and has the distinction of extending four rooms deep into the rock. The main room is set back about 13 feet from the face of the bluff, about 7 feet of this distance being occupied by a narrow passageway and the remainder by a cove. The depth from the face of the bluff to the back of the innermost chamber is 47 feet. The main room measures 16 feet in length and 11 feet in width, and its roof is less than 7 feet high in the center. Near its center and opposite the long passageway mentioned there is a fire-pit nearly 3 feet in diameter.

At the northeastern corner of the main room there is a wide opening leading into a room measuring 8 by 7 feet, with a floor raised 2 feet above that of the principal apartment. The roof of this chamber is but 4½ feet above the floor. Almost the whole eastern side of this room is occupied by a wide opening leading into another room of approximately the same size and shape. The roof of this room is only 3 feet 10 inches above the floor, and the floor is raised 6 inches above that on the west. In the northeastern corner there is a short narrow passageway leading into a small circular room, the fourth of the series, having a diameter of 4 feet. The roof of this apartment is only 3 feet above the floor.

In the southeastern corner of the main room there is a narrow passageway leading into a circular chamber about 8 feet in diameter. This chamber is connected with the second room of the series described by a passageway about 2 feet long, which opens into the southeastern corner of that room. This passageway, at its northern end, is 1½ feet below the room into which it opens. One of the most noticeable features about this group of rooms is the entire absence of the little nooks and pockets in the wall which are characteristic of these lodges, and which are very numerous in all the principal groups, noticeably in the group next described.

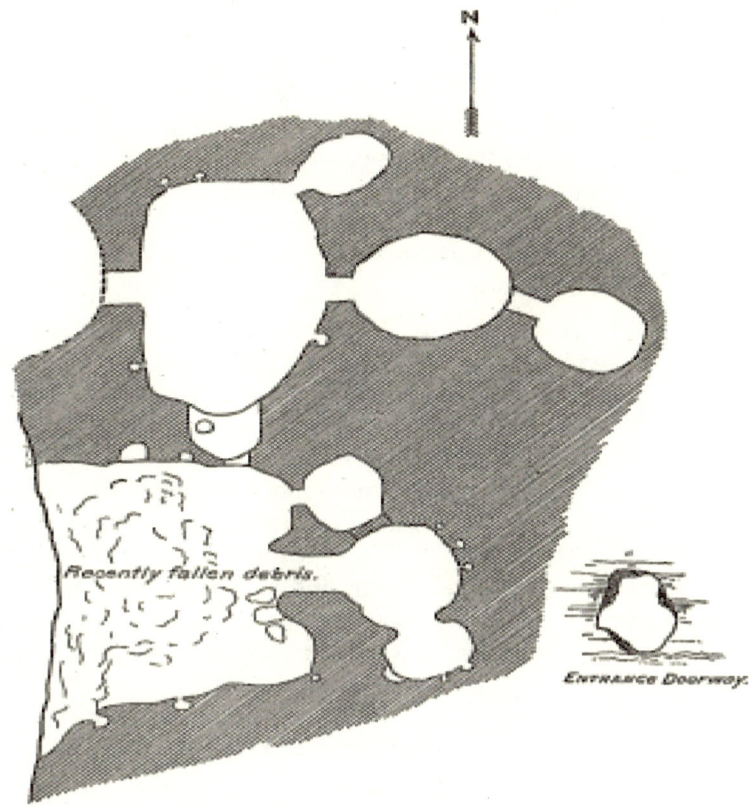

FIG. 298.—PLAN OF CAVATE LODGES, GROUP C.

At the point marked *C* on the map there is an elaborate group of chambers, consisting of two groups joined together and comprising altogether eight rooms. This is shown in plan in figure 298. The rock composing the front of the main room of the southern group has recently fallen, making a pile of debris about 4 feet high. The room originally measured about 12 by 22 feet. Its eastern side is occupied by a passageway leading into an adjoining chamber and by two shallow, roughly semi-circular coves, apparently the remains of former small rooms. Along the northern wall of the room there are two little nooks at the floor level, and along the southern wall there are four, one of them (shown on the plan) being dug out like a pit. The roof of the room was about 6 feet above the floor.

The passageway near the eastern side is 4½ feet long, and is 3½ feet wide—an unusual width. It opens into a roughly circular room, 8 feet in diameter, but with a roof only 3½ feet above the floor. Along the northeastern side of this room, there are three small pockets opening on the floor level. On the southern side of the room there is a wide opening into a small attached room, roughly oblong in shape and measuring about 6½ by 4½ feet. Along the southern wall of this little room there are two small pockets, and at the southwestern corner the rock has been cleared out to form a low cavity in the shape of a half dome. In the northwestern corner of the room there is another wide passage to a small room attached to the main room. This passage is now carefully sealed on its southern side with a slab of stone, plastered neatly so as to be hardly perceptible from the southern side. The room into which this passage opens on the north is attached to the northeastern corner of the main apartment by a narrow passage, 1½ feet wide and a foot long. It is roughly circular in shape, about 6 feet in diameter, and is the only chamber in the southern group which has no pockets or cubby-holes. Of these pockets there are no fewer than twelve in the southern group. Near the northern corner of the main room there is a doorway leading into a cove, which in turn opens into the main room of the northern group.

The main room of the northern group is setback about 9 feet from the face of the bluff, but is entered by a passageway about 3 feet long, the remainder of the distance consisting of a cove in the cliff. The room is 22 feet long and 13 feet wide and its roof is 6½ feet above the floor. In the southwestern corner there is a small pocket in the wall, and in the northwestern corner two others, all on the floor level. In the eastern side, however, there is a cubby-hole nearly 2 feet in diameter and about 2 feet above the floor. This is a rare feature. The southern end of the room opens into a kind of cove, raised 2 feet above the floor of the main room, and opening at its southern end into the main room of the southern group. In the floor of this cove there is a circular pit about 18 inches in diameter (marked in the plan, figure 298). Although resembling the fire holes already described, the position of the pit under consideration precludes use for that purpose; it was probably designed to contain water. At the northeastern corner of the principal apartment there is an oblong chamber or storage cist, measuring 6 feet by 7 feet.

Connected with the main room by a passageway 2 feet long cut in its eastern wall, there is an almost circular chamber 7 feet in diameter, and this in turn connects with another chamber beyond it by a passageway 2½ feet long and less than 2 feet wide. The roofs of the two chambers last mentioned are but 4½ and 4 feet, respectively, above the floor, and in none of the rooms of this group, except the main apartment, are pockets or niches found. The whole group extends back about 45 feet into the bluff.

BOWLDER-MARKED SITES.

Within the limits of the region here treated there are many hundreds of sites of structures and groups of rooms now marked only by lines of water-rounded bowlders. As a rule each site was occupied by only one or two rooms, although sometimes the settlement rose to the dignity of a village of considerable size. The rooms were nearly always oblong, similar in size and ground plan to the rooms composing the village ruins already described, but differing in two essential points, viz, character of site and character of the masonry. As a rule these remains are found on and generally near the edge of a low mesa or hill overlooking some area of tillable land, but they are by no means confined to such locations, being often found directly on the bottom land, still more frequently on the banks of dry washes at the points where they emerge from the hills, and sometimes on little islands or raised areas within the wash where every spring they must have been threatened with overflow or perhaps even overflowed. An examination of many sites leads to the conclusion that permanency was not an element of much weight in their selection.

Externally these bowlder-marked sites have every appearance of great antiquity, but all the evidence obtainable in regard to them indicates that they were connected with and inhabited at the same time as the other ruins in the region in which they are found. They are so much obliterated now, however, that a careful examination fails to determine in some cases whether the site in question was or was not occupied by a room or group of rooms, and there is a notable dearth of pottery fragments such as are so abundant in the ruins already described. Excavation in a large ruin of this type, however, conducted by some ranchmen living just above Limestone creek, yielded a considerable lot of pottery, not differing in kind from the fragments found in stone ruins so far as can be judged from description alone.

PLATE XXXIII. BOWLDER-MARKED SITE.

In the southern part of the region here treated bowlder-marked sites are more clearly marked and more easily distinguished than in the northern part, partly perhaps because in that section the normal ground surface is smoother than in the northern section and affords a greater contrast with the site itself. Plate XXXIII shows one of these bowlder-marked sites which occurs a little below Limestone creek, on the opposite or eastern side of the river. It is typical of many in that district. It will be noticed that the bowlders are but slightly sunk into the soil, and that the surface of the ground has been so slightly disturbed that it is practically level; there is not enough débris on the ground to raise the walls 2 feet. The illustration shows, in the middle distance, a considerable area of bottom land which the site overlooks. In plan this site shows a number of oblong rectangular rooms, the longer axes of which are not always parallel, the plan resembling very closely the smaller stone village ruins already described. It is probable that the lack of parallelism in the longer axes of the rooms is due to the same cause as in the village ruins, i.e., to the fact that the site was not all built up at one time.

The illustration represents only a part of an extensive series of wall remains. The series commences at the northern end of a mesa forming the eastern boundary of the Rio Verde and a little below a point opposite the mouth of Limestone creek. The ruins occur along the western rim of the mesa, overlooking the river and the bottom lands on the other side, and are now marked only by bowlders and a slight rise in the ground. But few lines of wall are visible, most of the ruins consisting only of a few bowlders scattered without system. From the northern end of the mesa, where the ruins commence, traces of walls can be seen extending due southward and at an angle of about 10° with the mesa edge for a distance of one-fourth of a mile. Beyond this, for half a mile or more southward, remains of single houses and small clusters occur, and these are found in less abundance to the southern edge of the mesa, where the ruin illustrated occurs. The settlement extended some distance east of the part illustrated, and also southward on the slope of the hill. Two well-marked lines of wall occur at the foot of the hill, on the flat bottom land, but the slopes of the hill are covered with bowlders and show no well-defined lines. Scattered about on the surface of the ground are some fragments of metates of coarse black basalt and some potsherds, but the latter are not abundant.

The bowlders which now mark these sites were probably obtained in the immediate vicinity of the points where they were used. The mesa on which the ruin occurs is a river terrace, constructed partly of these bowlders; they outcrop occasionally on its surface and show clearly in its sloping sides, and the washes that carry off the water falling on its surface are full of them.

In the northern end of the settlement there are faint traces of what may have been an irrigating ditch, but the topography is such that water could not be brought on top of the mesa from the river itself. At the southern end of the settlement, northeast of the point shown in the illustration, there are traces of a structure that may have been a storage reservoir. The surface of the mesa dips slightly southward, and the reservoir-like structure is placed at a point just above the head of a large wash, where a considerable part of the water that falls upon the surface of the mesa could be caught. It is possible that, commencing at the northern end of the settlement, a ditch extended completely through it, terminating in the storage reservoir at the southern end, and that this ditch was used to collect the surface water and was not connected with the river. A method of irrigation similar to this is practiced today by some of the Pueblo Indians, notably by the Hopi or Tusayan and by the Zuni. In the bottom land immediately south of the mesa, now occupied by several American families, there is a fine example of an aboriginal ditch, described later.

In the vicinity of the large ruin just above Limestone creek, previously described, the bowlder-marked sites are especially abundant. In the immediate vicinity of that ruin there are ten or more of them, and they are abundant all along the edge of the mesa forming the upper river terrace; in fact, they are found in every valley and on every point of mesa overlooking a valley containing tillable land.

It is probable that the bowlder-marked ruins are the sites of secondary and temporary structures, erected for convenience in working fields near to or overlooked by them and distant from the home pueblo. The character of the sites occupied by them and the plan of the structures themselves supports this hypothesis. That they were connected with the permanent stone villages is evident from their comparative abundance about each of the larger ones, and that they were constructed in a less substantial manner than the home pueblo is shown by the character of the remains.

It seems quite likely that only the lower course or courses of the walls of these dwellings were of bowlders, the superstructure being perhaps sometimes of earth (not adobe) but more probably often of the type known as "jacal"—upright slabs of wood plastered with mud. This method of construction was known to the ancient pueblo peoples and is used today to a considerable extent by the Mexican population of the southwest and to a less extent in some of the pueblos. No traces of this construction were found in the bowlder-marked sites, perhaps because no excavation was carried on; but it is evident that the rooms were not built of stone, and that not more than a small percentage could have been built of rammed earth or grout, as the latter, in disintegrating leaves well-defined mounds and lines of debris. It is improbable, moreover, that the structures were of brush plastered with mud, such as the Navajo hogan, as this method of construction is not well adapted to a rectangular ground plan, and if persistently applied would soon modify such a plan to a round or partially rounded one. Temporary brush structures would not require stone foundations, but structures composed of upright posts or slabs, filled in with brush and plastered with mud, and designed to last more than one farming season, would probably be placed on stone foundations, as the soil throughout most of the region in which these remains occur is very light, and a wooden structure placed directly on it would hardly survive a winter.

In the valley of the Rio Verde the profitable use of adobe at the present time is approximately limited northward by the thirty-fourth parallel, which crosses the valley a little below the mouth of Limestone creek. North of this latitude adobe is used less and less and where used requires more and more attention to keep in order, although on the high tablelands some distance farther northward it is again a suitable construction. South of the thirty-fourth parallel, however, adobe construction is well suited to the climate and in the valleys of Salt and Gila rivers it is the standard construction. Adobe construction (the use of sun-dried molded brick) was unknown to the ancient pueblo builders, but its aboriginal counterpart, rammed earth or pisé construction, such as that of the well known Casa Grande ruin on Gila river, acted in much the same way under climatic influences, and it is probable that its lack of suitability precluded its use in the greater part of the Verde valley. No walls of the type of those of the Casa Grande ruin have been found in the valley of the Verde, although abundant in the valleys of the Salt and Gila rivers, but it is possible that this method of construction was used in the southern part of the Verde region for temporary structures; in the northern part of that region its use even for that purpose was not practicable.

In this connection it should be noted that all the ruins herein described are of buildings of the northern type of aboriginal pueblo architecture and seem to be connected with the north rather than the south.

PLATE XXXIV. IRRIGATING DITCH ON THE LOWER VERDE.

IRRIGATING DITCHES AND HORTICULTURAL WORKS.

One of the finest examples of an aboriginal irrigating ditch that has come under the writer's notice occurs about 2 miles below the mouth of Limestone creek, on the opposite or eastern side of the river. At this point there is a large area of fertile bottom land, now occupied by some half dozen ranches, known locally as the Lower Verde settlement. The ditch extends across the northern and western part of this area. Plate XXXIV shows a portion of this ditch at a point about one eighth of a mile east of the river. Here the ditch is marked by a very shallow trough in the grass-covered bottom, bounded on either side by a low ridge of earth and pebbles. Plate XXXV shows the same ditch at a point about one-eighth of a mile above the last, where it was necessary to cut through a low ridge. North of this point the ditch can not be traced, but here it is about 40 feet above the river and about 10 feet above a modern (American) ditch. It is probable that the water was taken out of the river about 2 miles above this place, but the ditch was run on the sloping side of the mesa which has been recently washed out. No traces of the ditch were found east of the point shown in plate XXXIV, but as the modern acequia, which enters the valley nearly 10 feet below the ancient one, extends up the valley nearly to its head, there is no reason to suppose that the ancient ditch did not irrigate nearly the whole area of bottom land. The ancient ditch is well marked by two clearly defined lines of pebbles and small bowlders, as shown in the illustration. Probably these pebbles entered into its construction, as the modern ditch, washed out at its head and abandoned more than a year ago, shows no trace, of a similar marking.

PLATE XXXV. OLD IRRIGATING DITCH, SHOWING CUT
THROUGH LOW RIDGE.

A little west and south of the point shown in plate XXXIV the bottom land drops off by a low bench of 3 or 4 feet to a lower level or terrace, and this edge is marked for a distance of about a quarter of a mile by the remains of a stone wall or other analogous structure. This is located on the extreme edge of the upper bench and it is marked on its higher side by a very small elevation. On the outer or lower side it is more clearly visible, as the stones of which the wall was composed are scattered over the slope marking the edge of the upper bench. At irregular intervals along the wall there are distinct rectangular areas about the size of an ordinary pueblo room, i.e., about 8 by 10 and 10 by 12 feet.

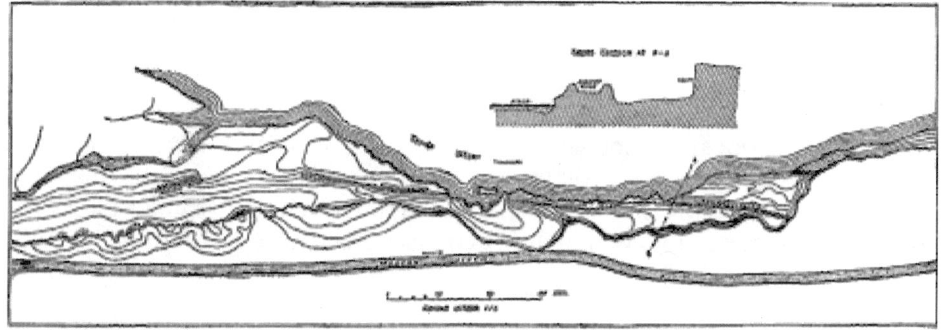

FIG. 299.—MAP OF AN ANCIENT IRRIGATING DITCH.

PLATE XXXVI. OLD DITCH NEAR VERDE, LOOKING WESTWARD.

In February, 1891, there was an exceptional flood in Verde river due to pro-longed hard rain. The river in some places rose nearly 20 feet, and at many points washed away its banks and changed the channel. The river rose on two occasions; during its first rise it cut away a considerable section of the bank near a point known as Spanish wash, about 3½ miles below Verde, exposing an ancient ditch. During its second rise it cut away still more of the bank and part of the ancient ditch exposed a few days before. The river here makes a sharp bend and flows a little north of east. The modern American ditch, which supplied all the bottom lands of the Verde west of the river, was ruined in this vicinity by the flood that uncovered the old ditch. Figure 299 is a map of the ancient ditch drawn in the field, with contours a foot apart, and showing also a section, on a somewhat larger scale, drawn through the points *A, B* on the map. Plate XXXVI is a view of the ditch look-ing westward across the point where it has been washed away, and plate XXXVII shows the eastern portion, where the ditch disappears under the bluff.

PLATE XXXVII. OLD DITCH NEAR VERDE, LOOKING EASTWARD.

The bank of the river at this point consists of a low sandy beach, from 10 to 50 feet wide, limited on the south by a vertical bluff 10 to 12 feet high and composed of sandy alluvial soil. This bluff is the edge of the bottom land before referred to, and on top is almost flat and covered with a growth of mesquite, some of the trees reaching a diameter of more than 3 inches. The American ditch, which is shown on the map, runs along the top of the bluff skirting its edge, and is about 14 feet above the river at its ordinary stage. The edge of the bluff is shown on the map by a heavy black line. It will be observed that the ancient ditch occurs on the lower flat, about 3 feet above the river at its ordinary stage, and its remains extend over nearly 500 feet. The line, however, is not a straight one, but has several decided bends. One of these occurs at a point just west of that shown in the section. About 80 feet east of that point the ditch makes another turn southward, and about 40 feet beyond strikes the face of the bluff almost at right angles and passes under it.

FIG. 300.—PART OF OLD IRRIGATING DITCH.

About 50 feet north of the main ditch, at the point where it passes under the bluff, there are the remains of another ditch, as shown on the map. This second ditch was about a foot higher than the main structure, or about 4 feet above the river; it runs nearly parallel with it for 30 feet and then passes into the bluff with a slight turn toward the north. It is about the same size as the main ditch, but its section is more evenly rounded. Figure 300 shows this ditch in section.

As already stated, the American ditch is about 14 feet above the river, while the ancient ditch is less than 4 feet above the water. This decided difference in level indicates a marked difference in the character of the river. The destruction of the modern ditch by the flood of 1891 is not the first mishap of that kind which has befallen the settlers. The ditch immediately preceding the current one passed nearly over the center of the ancient ditch, then covered by 10 feet or more of alluvial soil, and if a ditch were placed today on the level of the ancient structure it would certainly be destroyed every spring. The water that flowed through the modern ditch was taken from the river at a point about 3 miles farther northward, or just below Verde. The water for the ancient ditch must have been taken out less than a mile above the southern end of the section shown in the map.

At first sight it would appear that the ancient ditch antedated the deposit of alluvial soil forming the bottom land at this point, and this hypothesis is supported by several facts of importance. It is said that ten years ago the bottom land, whose edge now forms the bluff referred to, extended some 25 or 30 feet farther out, and that the river then flowed in a channel some 200 or 300 feet north of the present one. Be this as it may, the bottom land now presents a fairly continuous surface, from the banks of the river to the foothills that limit the valley on the west and south, and it is certain that this bottom land extended over the place occupied by the ancient ditch; nor is it to be supposed that the ancient ditches ended abruptly at the point where they now enter the bluff. The curves in the line of the ancient ditch might indicate that it was constructed along the slope of a hill, or on an uneven surface, as a deep excavation in fairly even ground would naturally be made in a straight line.

PLATE XXXVIII. BLUFF OVER ANCIENT DITCH, SHOWING GRAVEL STRATUM.

The face of the bluff shows an even deposit of sand, without apparent stratification, except here and there a thin layer or facing of mud occurs, such as covers the bottom of the ancient ditch and also of the modern ditch. Singularly enough, however, over the ancient ditch, about 5 feet above its bottom, there is a stratum of sand and gravel, and on top, within a few inches of the surface of the ground, a thin stratum of mud. This mud stratum extends only about 8 feet horizontally and is slightly hollowed, with its lowest part over the center of the ditch. The gravel stratum also was laid down over the ditch, is tilted slightly southward and occurs in two layers, together about a foot thick. It first appears a few feet south of the point where the main ditch enters the bluff and over the ditch both layers are distinctly marked, as shown in plate XXXVIII. Both layers are clearly marked to a distance of 4 feet north of the northern side of the main ditch; here the lower layer thins out, but the upper layer continues faintly marked almost to the edge of the small ditch. At this point the gravel stratum becomes pronounced again and continues over the small ditch, almost pure gravel in places, with a decided dip westward. At a point just beyond the northern side of the small ditch the gravel layer disappears entirely.

The occurrence of this gravel in the way described seems to indicate that the ditch was built along the slope of a low hill forming the edge of the bottom land at that time, and that subsequently detritus was deposited above it and over the adjacent bottom land forming a smooth ground surface. Against this hypothesis it must be stated that no evidence whatever was found of more than a single deposit of sandy loam, although the exposures are good; but perhaps were an examination made by a competent geologist some such evidence might be developed.

There is one fact that should not be lost sight of in the discussion, viz, the very low elevation of the ditch above the river. The Verde is, as already stated, a typical mountain stream, with an exceptionally high declivity, and consequently it is rapidly lowering its bed. If, as already conjectured, the water for the ancient ditch was taken from the river but a short distance above the point where remains of the ditch are now found—and this assumption seems well supported by the character of the adjacent topography—the slight elevation of the bed of the ditch above the river would indicate that, in the first place, the ditch was located, as already suggested, along the slope of a hill, and in the second place, that the ditch was built at a period of no great antiquity. The occurrence of the high bluff under which the ditch now passes does not conflict with this suggestion, for the deposition of the material composing it and its erosion into its present form and condition may be the result of decades rather than of centuries of work by a stream like the Verde, and certainly a hundred, or at most a hundred and fifty years would suffice to accomplish it. At the present time a few floods deposit an amount of material equal to that under discussion, and if subsequently the river changed its channel, as it does at a dozen different points every spring, a few decades only would be required to cover the surface with grass and bushes, and in short, to form a bottom land similar to that now existing over the ancient ditch.

In conclusion it should be noted, in support of the hypothesis that the ditch was built before the material composing the bluff was laid down, that immediately under the ditch there is a stratum of hard adobe-like earth, quite different from the sand above it and from the material of which the bluff is composed. This stratum is shown clearly in plate XXXVIII.

The hypothesis which accords best with the evidence now in hand is that which assumes that the ditch was taken out of the river but a short distance above the point illustrated, and that it was built on the slope of a low hill, or on a nearly flat undulating bottom land, before the material composing the present bottom or river terrace was deposited, and that the ditch, while it may be of considerable antiquity, is not necessarily more than a hundred or a hundred and fifty years old; in other words, we may reach a fairly definite determination of its minimum but not of its maximum antiquity.

On the southern side of Clear creek, about a mile above its mouth, there are extensive horticultural works covering a large area of the terrace or river bench. These have already been alluded to in the description of the village ruin overlooking them, but there are several features which are worthy a more detailed description. For a distance of 2 miles east and west along the creek, and perhaps half a mile north and south, there are traces of former works pertaining to horticulture, including irrigating ditches, "reservoirs," farming outlooks, etc.

PLATE XXXIX. ANCIENT DITCH AND HORTICULTURAL WORKS ON CLEAR CREEK.

At the eastern end of these works, about 3 miles above the mouth of Clear creek, the main ditch, after running along the slope of the hill for some distance, comes out on top of the mesa or terrace nearly opposite the Morris place. The water was taken from the creek but a short distance above, hardly more than half a mile. West of the point where the ditch comes out on the mesa top, all traces of it disappear, but they are found again at various points on the terrace. Plate XXXIX shows a portion of the terrace below and opposite the rectangular ruin previously described. In the distant foreground the light line indicates a part of the ancient ditch. Plate XL shows the same ditch at a point half a mile below the last, where it rounds a knoll. In the distance is the flat-topped hill or mesa on which the rectangular ruin previously described is located. About a hundred yards southeast of this point further traces of the ditch may be seen, and connected with it at that point are a number of rectangular areas, which were cultivated patches when the ditch was in use.

PLATE XL. ANCIENT DITCH AROUND A KNOLL, CLEAR CREEK.

The whole surface of the terrace within the limits described is covered by small water-worn bowlders scattered so thickly over it that travel is seriously impeded. In many parts of it these bowlders are arranged so as to inclose small rectangular areas, and these areas are connected with the old ditch just described. Plate XXXIX shows something of this surface character; and in the right hand portion of it may be seen some of the rows of bowlders forming the rectangular areas. The rows which occur at right angles to the ditch are much more clearly marked than those parallel to it, and the longer axes of the rectangular areas are usually also at right angles to the ditch line. On the ground these traces of inclosures can hardly be made out, but from an elevated point, such as the mesa on which, the rectangular ruin overlooking these works is located, they show very clearly and have the appearance of windrows. Traces of these horticultural works would be more numerous, and doubtless more distinct, were it not that a considerable part of the area formerly under cultivation has been picked over by the modern settlers in this region, and immense quantities of stone have been removed and used in the construction of fences. This has not been done, however, in such a manner as to leave the ground entirely bare, yet bare areas occur here and there over the surface, where doubtless once existed a part of the general scheme of horticultural works.

PLATE XLI. ANCIENT WORK ON CLEAR CREEK.

One such bare area occurs close to the edge of the terrace about a mile and a half above the mouth of the creek. In its center is a structure called for convenience a reservoir, although it is by no means certain that it was used as such. It occurs about 100 yards from the creek, opposite the Wingfield place, and consists of a depression surrounded by an elevated rim. It is oval, measuring 108 feet north and south and 72 feet east and west from rim to rim. The crown of the rim is 5 feet 8 inches above the bottom of the depression and about 3 feet above the ground outside. The rim is fairly continuous, except at points on the northern and southern sides, where there are slight depressions, and these depressions are further marked by extra large bowlders. At its lowest points, however, the rim is over 2 feet above the ground, which slopes away from it for some distance in every direction. Plate XLI shows the eastern side of the depression; the large tree in the middle distance is on the bank of Clear creek and below the terrace. Plate XLII shows the northern gateway or dip in the rim, looking southward across the depression. The large bowlders previously referred to can be clearly seen. A depression similar to this occurs on the opposite side of the valley, about half a mile from the river. In this case it is not marked by bowlders or stones of any description, but is smooth and rounded, corresponding to the surface of the ground in its vicinity. In the latter as in the former case, the depression occurs on a low knoll or swell in the bottom land, and the surface of the ground slopes gently away from it for some distance in every direction.

PLATE XLII. GATEWAY TO ANCIENT WORK, CLEAR CREEK.

The purpose of these depressions is not at all clear, and although popularly known as reservoirs it is hardly possible that they were used as such. The capacity of the Clear creek depression is about 160,000 gallons, or when two-thirds full, which would be the limit of its working capacity, about 100,000 gallons. The minimum rate of evaporation in this region in the winter months is over 3 inches per month, rising in summer to 10 inches or more, so that in winter the loss of water stored in this depression would be about 10,000 gallons a month, while in summer it might be as high as 35,000 or even 40,000 gallons a month. It follows, therefore, that even if the reservoir were filled to its full working capacity in winter and early spring it would be impossible to hold the water for more than two months and retain enough at the end of that time to make storing worth while. It has been already stated, however, that these depressions are situated on slight knolls and that the land falls away from them in every direction. As no surface drainage could be led into them, and as there is no trace on the ground of a raised ditch discharging into them, they must have been filled, if used as reservoirs, from the rain which fell within the line that circumscribes them. The mean annual rainfall (for over seventeen years) at Verde, a few miles farther northward in the same valley, is 11.44 inches, with a maximum annual fall of 27.27 inches and a minimum of 4.80 inches. The mean annual fall (for over twenty-one years) at Fort McDowell, near the mouth of the Rio Verde, is 10-54 inches, with a maximum of 20.0 inches and a minimum of 4.94 inches.[8]

---

[8] Report on Rainfall (Pacific coast and western states and territories), Signal Office U.S. War Dept., Senate Ex. Doc. 91, 50th Cong., 1st Sess., Washington, 1889; pp. 70-73 (Errata, p. 4).

If these depressions were used as reservoirs it is a fair presumption that the bottoms were plastered with clay, so that there would be no seepage and the only loss would be by evaporation. Yet this loss, in a dry and windy climate such as that of the region here treated, would be sufficient to render impracticable a storage reservoir of a cross section and a site like the one under discussion. Most of the rainfall is in the winter months, from December to March, and it would require a fall of over 12 inches during those months to render the reservoir of any use in June; it would certainly be of no use in July and August, at the time when water is most needed, save in exceptional years with rainfall much in excess of the mean.

On the other hand, there is the hypothesis that these depressions represent house structures; but if so these structures are anomalous in this region. The contour of the ground does not support the idea of a cluster of rooms about a central court, nor does the débris bear it out. Mr. F. H. Cushing has found depressions in the valleys of Salt and Gila rivers somewhat resembling these in form and measurement, and situated always on the outskirts of the sites of villages. Excavations were made, and as the result of these he came to the conclusion that the depressions were the remains of large council chambers, as the floors were hard, plastered with mud, and dish-shaped, with a fire-hole in the center of each; and no pottery or implements or remains of any kind were found except a number of "sitting stones." Mr. Cushing found traces of upright logs which formed the outer wall of the structure; he inferred from the absence of drainage channels that the structure was roofed, and as the ordinary method of roofing is impracticable on the scale of these structures, he supposed that a method similar to that used by the Pima Indians in roofing their granaries was employed, the roof being of a flattened dome shape and composed of grass or reeds, formed in a continuous coil and covered with earth. If the depressions under discussion, however, are the remains of structures such as these described, they form a curious anomaly in this region, for, as has been already stated, the affinities of the remains of this region are with the northern architectural types, and not at all with those of the southern.

There is a third hypothesis which, though not supported by direct evidence, seems plausible. It is that the depression of Clear creek, and perhaps also the one on the opposite side of the Verde, were thrashing floors. This hypothesis accords well with the situation of these depressions upon the tillable bottom lands, and with their relation to the other remains in their vicinity; and their depth below the surface of the ground would be accounted for, under the assumption here made of their use, by the high and almost continuous winds of the summer in this region. Perhaps the slight depressions at the northern and southern side of the oval were the gateways through which the animals which trampled the straw or the men who worked the flails passed in and out. Whether used in this way or not, these depressions would be, under the assumption that the bottom was plastered with mud, not only practicable, but even desirable thrashing floors, as the grain would be subjected during thrashing to a partial winnowing. This suggestion would also account for the comparatively clean ground surface about the depressions and for their location on slightly elevated knolls.

PLATE XLIII. SINGLE-ROOM REMAINS ON CLEAR CREEK.

Scattered over the whole area formerly under cultivation along Clear creek are the remains of small, single rooms, well marked on the ground, but without any standing wall remaining. These remains are scattered indiscriminately over the terrace without system or arrangement; they are sometimes on the flat, sometimes on slight knolls. They number altogether perhaps forty or fifty. Plate XLIII shows an example which occurs on a low knoll, shown also in plate XL; it is typical of these remains. It will be noticed that the masonry was composed of river bowlders not dressed or prepared in any way, and that the débris on the ground would raise the walls scarcely to the height of a single low story.

The location of these remains, their relation to other remains in the vicinity, and their character all support the conclusion that they were small temporary shelters or farming outlooks, occupied only during the season when the fields about them were cultivated and during the gathering of the harvest, as is the case with analogous structures used in the farming operations among the pueblos of to-day. Their number and distribution do not necessarily signify that all the terrace was under cultivation at one time, although there is a fair presumption that the larger part of it was, and the occurrence of the ditch at both the upper and the lower ends of the area strengthens this conclusion.

As it is impossible that an area so large as this should be cultivated by the inhabitants of one village, it is probable that a number of villages combined in the use of this terrace for their horticultural operations; and, reasoning from what we know to have been the case in other regions, it is further probable that this combination resulted in endless contention, and strife, and perhaps finally to the abandonment of these fields if not of this region. The rectangular ruin already illustrated is situated on a hill south of the terrace and overlooks it from that direction; on the opposite side of Clear creek, on the hill bounding the valley on the north, there are the remains of a large stone village which commanded an outlook over the terraces in question; and a little farther up the creek, on the same side and similarly situated, there was another village which also overlooked them. There were doubtless other villages and small settlements whose remains are not now clearly distinguishable, and it is quite probable that some of the inhabitants of the large villages in the vicinity, like those near Verde, hardly 3 miles northward, had a few farming houses and some land under cultivation on this terrace.

Thus it will be seen that there was no lack of cultivators for all the tillable land on the terrace, and there is no reason to suppose that the period when the land was under cultivation, and the period when the villages overlooking it were occupied, were not identical, and that the single-house remains scattered over the terrace were not built and occupied at the same period. The relation of the stone villages to the area formerly cultivated, the relation of the single-room remains to the area immediately about them, the character of the remains, and the known methods of horticulture followed by the Pueblo Indians, all support the conclusion that these remains were not only contemporaneous but also related to one another.

STRUCTURAL CHARACTERISTICS.
MASONRY AND OTHER DETAILS.

The masonry of the stone villages throughout all the region here treated is of the same type, although there are some variations. It does not compare with the fine work found on the San Juan and its tributaries, although belonging to that type—the walls being composed of two faces with rubble filling, and the interstices of the large stones being filled or chinked with spalls. This chinking is more pronounced and better done in the northern part of the region than in the south.

PLATE XLIV. BOWLDER FOUNDATIONS NEAR LIMESTONE CREEK.

PLATE XLV. MASONRY OF RUIN NEAR LIMESTONE CREEK.

The rock employed depended in all cases on the immediate environments of the site of the village, the walls being composed in some cases of slabs of limestone, in other cases of river bowlders only, and in still others of both in combination. The walls of the large ruin near Limestone creek were composed of rude slabs of limestone with an intermixture of bowlders. The bowlders usually occur only in the lower part of the wall, near the ground, and in several cases, where nothing exists of the wall above the surface of the ground, the remains consist entirely of bowlders. A good example of this peculiarity of construction is shown in plate XLIV, and plate XLV shows the character of stone employed and also a section of standing wall on the western side of the village. A section of standing wall near the center of the ruin is illustrated in plate XIII. It will be noticed that some of the walls shown in this illustration are chinked, but to a very slight extent. The wall represented in plate XLV has slabs of limestone set on edge. This feature is found also in other ruins in this region, notably in those opposite Verde, though it seems to be more used in the south than in the north. An example occurring in the ruin opposite Verde is shown in plate XLVI. In this case chinking is more pronounced; the walls are from 2 to 2½ feet thick, built in the ordinary way with two faces and an interior filling, but the stones are large and the filling is almost wholly adobe mortar. The two faces are tied together by extra long stones which occasionally project into the back of one or the other face.

PLATE XLVI. MASONRY OF RUIN OPPOSITE VERDE.

The western cluster of the ruin last mentioned, shown on the ground plan (plate XVII), has almost all its walls still standing, and the masonry, while of the same general character as that of the main cluster, is better executed. The stones composing the walls are smaller than those in the main cluster and more uniform in size, and the interstices are carefully chinked. The chinking is distinctive in that spalls were not used, but more or less flattened river pebbles. The different color and texture of these pebbles make them stand out from the wall distinctly, giving quite an ornamental effect.

PLATE XLVII. STANDING WALLS OPPOSITE VERDE.

That portion of the standing wall of the ruin opposite Verde, which occurs in the saddle northeastward from the main cluster, shown on the plan in plate XVII, represents the best masonry found in this region. As elsewhere stated, this was probably the last part of the village to be built. These walls are shown in plate XLVII. It will be noticed that the stones are of very irregular shape, rendering a considerable amount of chinking necessary to produce even a fair result, and that the stones are exceptionally large. The masonry of this village is characterized by the use of stones larger than common, many of them being larger than one man can carry and some of them even larger than two men can handle.

All the larger and more important ruins of this region are constructed of limestone slabs, sometimes with bowlders. The smaller ruins, on the other hand, were built usually of river bowlders, sometimes with an intermixture of slabs of limestone and sandstone but with a decided preponderance of river bowlders. This would seem to suggest that this region was gradually populated, and that the larger structures were the last ones built. This suggestion has been already made in the discussion of the ground plans, and it is, moreover, in accord with the history of the pueblo-builders farther northward, notably that of the Hopi.

PLATE XLVIII. MASONRY OF RUIN AT MOUTH OF THE EAST
VERDE.

Plate XXI illustrates a type of bowlder masonry which occurs on Clear creek; plate XLVIII shows the masonry of the ruin at the mouth of the East Verde, and plate XVI shows that of a ruin at the month of Fossil creek. In all these examples the stone composing the walls was derived either from the bed of an adjacent stream or from the ground on which they were built, and was used without any preparation whatever; yet in the better examples of this type of masonry a fairly good result was obtained by a careful selection of the stones. A still ruder type of masonry sometimes found in connection with village ruins is shown in figure 290. This, however, was used only as in the example illustrated, for retaining walls to trails or terraces, or analogous structures.

In a general way it may be stated that the masonry of the village ruins of this region is much inferior to that of the San Juan region, and in its rough and unfinished surfaces, in the use of an inferior material close at hand rather than a better material a short distance away, and in the ignorance on the part of the builders of many constructive devices and expedients employed in the best examples of pueblo masonry, the work of this region may be ranked with that of the Tusayan—in other words, at the lower end of the scale.

FIG. 301.—WALLED FRONT CAVATE LODGES.

There is but little masonry about the cavate lodges, and that is rude in character. As elsewhere stated, walled fronts are exceptional in this region, and where they occur the work was done very roughly. Figure 301 shows an example that occurs in the group of cavate lodges already described. It will be noticed that little selection has been exercised in the stones employed, and that an excess of mortar has been used to fill in the large interstices. Figure 290 (p. 221), which shows a storage cist attached to the group of cavate lodges, marked D on the map (plate XXV), exhibits the same excessive use of adobe or mud plastering. At several other points in the area shown on this map there are short walls, sometimes inside the lodges, sometimes outside. In all cases, however, they are rudely constructed and heavily plastered with mud; in short, the masonry of the cavate lodges exhibits an ignorance fully equal to that of the stone villages, while the execution is, if anything, ruder. It is singular that, notwithstanding the excessive use of mud mortar and mud plastering in the few walls that are found there, such plastering was almost never used on the walls in the interiors of the lodges, perhaps because no finer finish than the rough surface of the rock was considered desirable.

The cavate lodges seem to have been excavated without the aid of other tools than a rough maul or a piece of stone held in the hand, and such a tool is well adapted to the work, since a blow on the surface of the rock is sufficient to bring off large slabs. Notwithstanding the rude tools and methods, however, some of the work is quite neat, especially in the passageways (which are often 3 or 4 feet long and quite narrow) and in the smaller chambers. In the excavation of these chambers benches were left at convenient places along the wall and niches and cubby-holes were cut, so that in the best examples of cavate lodges the occupants, it would seem, were more comfortable, so far as regards their habitation, than the ordinary Pueblo Indian of today, and better supplied with the conveniences of that method of living. It should be stated in this connection, however, that although the group of cavate lodges gives an example of an extensive work well carried out, the successful carrying out of that work does not imply either a large population or a high degree of skill; the only thing necessary was time, and the amount of time necessary for the work is not nearly so great, in proportion to the population housed, as was required for the better types of pueblo work in the San Juan country (the village ruins of the Chaco canyon for example), and probably no more than would be required for the construction of rooms of equal size and of the rather poor grade of work found in this region.

Although no examples of interior wall-plastering were found in the group of cavate lodges described, such work has been found in neighboring lodges; and in this group plastered floors are quite common. The object of plastering the floors was to secure a fairly even surface such as the soft rock did not provide, and this was secured not by the application of layers of clay but by the use of clay here and there wherever needed to bring the surface up to a general level, and the whole surface was subsequently finished. This final finishing was sometimes omitted, and many floors are composed partly of the natural rock and partly of clay, the latter frequently in spots and areas of small size.

The floors were often divided into a number of sections by low ridges of clay, sometimes 8 inches broad. These ridges are shown on the ground plans (figures 294 to 298, and in plate XXV). Their purpose is not clear, although it can readily be seen that in such domestic operations as sorting grain they would be useful.

DOOR AND WINDOW OPENINGS.

The masonry of this region was so roughly and carelessly executed that little evidence remains in the stone villages of such details of construction as door and window openings. Destruction of the walls seems to have commenced at these openings, and while there are numerous standing walls, some with a height of over 10 feet, no perfect example of a door or window opening was found. It is probable that the methods employed were similar or analogous to those used to-day by the Hopi, and that the wooden lintel and stone jamb was the standard type.

PLATE XLIX. DOORWAY TO CAVATE LODGE.

FIG. 302.—BOWLDERS IN FOOTWAY, CAVATE LODGES.

In the cavate lodges window openings are not found; there is but one opening, the doorway, and this is of a pronounced and peculiar type. As a rule these doorways are wider at the top than at the bottom and there are no corners, the opening roughly approximating the shape of a pear with the smaller end downward. The upper part of the opening consists always of the naked rock, but the lower part is generally framed with slabs of sandstone. Plate XLIX shows an example that occurs in the upper tier of lodges at its eastern end. The floor of this lodge is about 2 feet above the bench from which it was entered, and this specimen fails to show a feature which is very common in this group—a line of water-worn bowlders extending from the exterior to the interior of the lodges through the doorway and arranged like stepping stones. This feature is shown in figure 302, which represents the doorway of group E, shown on the general map (plate XXV) and on the detailed plan, figure 297. Figure 303 shows a type in which the framing is extended up on one side nearly to the top, while on the other side it extends only to half the height of the opening, which above the framing is hollowed out to increase its width. This example occurs near that shown in plate XLIX, and the floor of the chamber is raised about 2 feet above the bench from which it is entered. The illustration gives a view from the interior, looking out, and the large opening on the right was caused by the comparatively recent breaking out of the wall. Figure 303 shows the doorway to the group of chambers marked E on the general map, an interior view of which is shown in figure 302. In this example the obvious object of the framing was to reduce the size of the opening, and to accomplish this the slabs were set out 10 or 12 inches from the rock forming the sides of the opening, and the intervening space was filled in with rubble. Plate plate XXXII, which shows the interior of the main room in group D, shows also the large doorway on the north.

FIG. 303.—FRAMED DOORWAY, CAVATE LODGES.

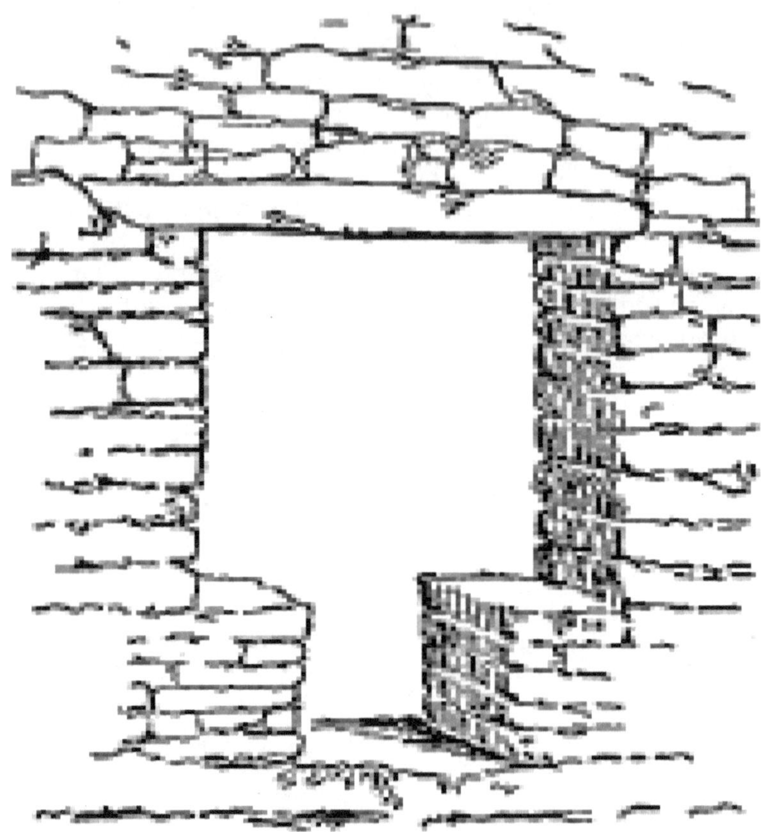

FIG. 304.—NOTCHED DOORWAY IN CANYON DE CHELLY.

It will be noticed that these doorways all conform to one general plan and that this plan required an opening considerably larger in its upper third than in the lower two-thirds of its height. This requirement seems to be the counterpart or analogue of the notched doorway, which is the standard type in the cliff ruins of Canyon de Chelly and other regions, and still very common in Tusayan (Moki). Figure 304 shows a notched doorway in Canyon de Chelly and figure 305 gives an example of the same type of opening in Tusayan. The object of this peculiar shape in the regions mentioned has been well established,[9] and there is no reason to suppose that similar conditions and a similar object would not produce a similar result here. This type of opening had its origin in the time when the pueblo builders had no means, other than blankets, of temporarily closing door openings and when all the supplies of the village were brought in on the backs of the inhabitants. In order to secure protection against cold and storm the opening was made of the smallest possible size consistent with its use, and the upper part of the opening was made larger in order to permit the introduction of back loads of faggots and other necessaries. This purpose would be almost as well served by the openings

[9] A Study of Pueblo Architecture, by Victor Mindeleff: 8th. Ann. Rep. Bur. Eth. for 1886-1887; Washington, 1891, pp. 1-228.

of the cavate lodges as by the notched doorway, and at the same time the smallest possible opening was exposed to the weather. The two types of openings seem simply to be two different methods of accomplishing the same purpose—one in solid rock, the other in masonry. That it was considered desirable to reduce the openings as much as possible is evident from the employment of framing slabs in the lower portions, reducing the width of that part generally to less than a foot, while the upper portions are usually 3 feet and more in width, and the absence of framing slabs in the upper part of the openings was probably due to their use as suggested; no slabs could be attached with sufficient firmness to resist the drag of a back load of wood, for example, forced between them. The strict confinement of door openings to one type suggests a short, rather than a long, occupancy of the site under discussion, a suggestion which is borne out by other details; and this unity of design renders it difficult to form a conclusion as to the relative age of the two types of openings under discussion. So far as the evidence goes, however, it supports the conclusion that the doorways of the cavate lodges were derived from a type previously developed, and that the idea has been modified and to some extent adapted to a different environment; for if the idea had been developed in the cavate lodges there would be a much greater number of variations than we find in fact. There can be no doubt, however, that the cavate lodge doorways represent an earlier type in development, if not in time, than the notched doorways of Tusayan.

FIG. 305.—NOTCHED DOORWAY IN TUSAYAN.

CHIMNEYS AND FIREPLACES.

Nowhere in the village ruins or in the cavate lodges of the lower Verde were any traces of chimneys or other artificial smoke exits found. The village ruins are too much broken down to permit definite statement of the means employed for smoke exits, but had the inhabitants employed such exits as are in use in the pueblos today some evidence of them would remain. Probably there was no other exit than the door, and perhaps trapdoors or small openings in the roofs, such as were formerly employed in the inhabited pueblos, according to their traditions. In the cavate lodges no exit other than the door was possible, and many of them are found with their walls much blackened by smoke.

The fireplaces or fire holes of the cavate lodges have already been alluded to, and one of the best examples found is illustrated in plate XXXII, and the location of a number of others is shown on the general plan. These fireplaces are located not in the center of the chamber, but near the principal doorway, and doubtless the object of this location was to facilitate the escape of the smoke. Fire holes were never located in interior rooms. The fireplace illustrated in plate XXXII has been already described (p. 227); it was excavated in the solid rock of the floor and was lined with fragments of pottery laid in mud mortar as closely as their shape would permit. A part of this pottery lining can be seen in the illustration. When the room was cleared out the fire hole was found to be about half full of fine ashes.

CONCLUSIONS.

The ruins of the lower Verde valley represent a comparatively late period in the history of the Pueblo tribes. The period of occupancy was not a long one and the population was never large, probably not exceeding at any time 800 or 1,000 souls, possibly less than 700; nor were the dwellings in that region all occupied at the same time.

There is no essential difference, other than those due to immediate environment, between the architecture of the lower Verde region and that of the more primitive types found in other regions, Tusayan for example. The Verde architecture is, however, of a more purely aboriginal type than that of any modern pueblo, and the absence of introduced or foreign ideas is its chief characteristic. There are no chimneys, no adobe walls, no constructive expedients other than aboriginal and rather primitive ones. The absence of circular kivas[10] or sacred council chambers is noteworthy.

The circular kiva is a survival of an ancient type—a survival supported by all the power of religious feeling and the conservatism in religious matters characteristic of savage and barbarous life; and while most of the modern pueblos have at the present time rectangular kivas, such, for example, as those at Tusayan, at Zuñi, and at Acoma, there is no doubt that the circular form is the more primitive and was formerly used by some tribes which now have only the rectangular form. Still the abandonment of the circular and the adoption of the rectangular form, due to expediency and the breaking down of old traditions, was a very gradual process and proceeded at a different rate in different parts of the country. At the time of the Spanish conquest the prevailing form in the old province of Cibola was rectangular, although the circular kiva was not entirely absent; while, on the other hand, in the cliff ruins of Canyon de Chelly, whose date is partly subsequent to the sixteenth century, the circular kiva is the prevailing, if not the exclusive form. But notwithstanding this the Hopi Indians of Tusayan, to whom many of the Canyon de Chelly ruins are to be attributed, today have not a single circular kiva. The reason for this radical departure from the old type is a simple one, and to be found in the single term environment. The savage is truly a child of nature and almost completely under its sway. A slight difference in the geologic formations of two regions will produce a difference in the arts of the inhabitants of those regions, provided the occupancy be a long one. In the case of the Tusayan kivas the rectangular form was imposed on the builders by the character of the sites they occupied. The

[10] As this term has been already defined, it is here used without further explanation. For a full discussion of these structures, see "A Study of Pueblo Architecture," by Victor Mindeleff, in 8th. Ann. Rep. Bur. Eth., 1886-87, Washington, 1891.

requirement that the kiva should be under ground, or partly under ground, was a more stringent one than that it should be circular, and with the rude appliances at their command the Tusayan builders could accomplish practically nothing unless they utilized natural cracks and fissures in the rocks. Hence the abandonment of the circular form and also of the more essential requirement, that the kiva should be inclosed within the walls of the village or within a court; the Tusayan kivas are located indiscriminately in the courts and on the outskirts of the village, wherever a suitable site was found, some of them being placed at a considerable distance from the nearest house.

It will be seen, therefore, that it is impossible to base any chronologic conclusions on the presence or absence of this feature, notwithstanding the undoubted priority of the circular form, except in so far as these conclusions are limited to some certain region or known tribal stock. If it be assumed that the Verde ruins belong to the Tusayan, and all the evidence in hand favors that assumption, the conclusion follows that they should be assigned to a comparatively late period in the history of that tribe.

That the period of occupancy of the lower Verde valley was not a long one is proved by the character of the remains and by what we know of the history of the pueblo-building tribes. There are no very large areas of tillable land on the lower Verde and not a large number of small ones, and aside from these areas the country is arid and forbidding in the extreme. Such a country would be occupied only as a last resort, or temporarily during the course of a migration. The term migration, however, must not be taken in the sense in which it has been applied to European stocks, a movement of people en masse or in several large groups. Migration as used here, and as it generally applies to the Pueblo Indians, means a slow gradual movement, generally without any definite and ultimate end in view. A small section of a village, generally a gens or a subgens, moves away from the parent village, perhaps only a few miles. At another time another section moves to another site, at still another time another section moves, and so on. These movements are not possible where outside hostile pressure is strong, and if such pressure is long continued it results in a reaggregation of the various scattered settlements into one large village. Such in brief is the process which is termed migration, and which has covered the southwest with thousands of village ruins. Of course larger movements have occurred and whole villages have been abandoned in a day, but as a rule the abandonment of villages was a gradual process often consuming years.

Before the archeologic investigation of the pueblo region commenced and when there was little knowledge extant by which travelers could check their conclusions, the immense number of ruins in that region was commonly attributed to an immense population, some writers placing the number as high as 500,000. Beside this figure the present population, about 9,000, is so insignificant that it is hardly surprising that the ancient and modern villages were separated and attributed to different tribal stocks.

The process briefly sketched above explains the way in which village ruins have their origin; a band of 500 village-building Indians might leave the ruins of fifty villages in the course of a single century. It is very doubtful whether the total number of Pueblo Indians ever exceeded 30,000. This is the figure stated by Mr. A. F. Bandelier, whose intimate acquaintance with the eastern part of the pueblo region gives his opinion great weight. The apparently trifling causes which sometimes result in the abandonment of villages have been already alluded to.

The lower Verde forms no exception to the general rule sketched above. Scattered along the river, and always located on or immediately adjacent to some area of tillable land, are found many small ruins, typical examples of which have been described in detail. These form the subordinate settlements whose place in the general scheme has been indicated. The masonry is generally of river bowlders only, not dressed or prepared in any way. The number of these settlements is no greater than would be required for one complete cycle or period, although the evidence seems to support the hypothesis that the movement commenced in the northern part of the region and proceeded southward in two or perhaps three separate steps. It is possible, however, that the movement was in the other direction. This question can be settled only by a thorough examination of the regions to the north and south.

There are two, possibly three, points in the region discussed where a stand was made and the various minor settlements were abandoned, the inhabitants congregating into larger bands and building a larger village for better defense against the common foe. These are located at the extreme northern and southern limits of the region treated, opposite Verde and near Limestone creek, and possibly also at an intermediate point, the limestone ruin above Fossil creek. These more important ruins are all built of limestone slabs, and the sites are carefully selected. The internal evidence supports the conclusion that the movement was southward and that in the large ruin near Limestone creek the inhabitants of the lower Verde valley had their last resting place before they were absorbed by the population south of them, or were driven permanently from this region. The strong resemblance of the ground plan of this village to that of Zuñi has been already commented on, and it is known that Zuñi was produced in the way stated, by the inhabitants of the famous "seven cities of Cibola," except that in this case Zuñi was the second site adopted, the aggregation into one village, or more properly a number of villages on one site, having taken place a few years before. The fact that Zuñi dates only from the beginning of the last century should not be lost sight of in this discussion.

The inhabitants of the Verde valley were an agricultural people, and even in the darkest days of their history, when they were compelled to abandon the minor settlements, they still relied on horticulture for subsistence, and to a certain extent the defense motive was subordinated to the requirements of this method of life. There can be no doubt that the hostile pressure which produced the larger villages was Indian, probably the Apache and Walapai, who were in undisputed possession at the time of the American advent, and but little doubt that this pressure consisted not of regular invasions and set sieges, but of sudden raids and descents upon the fields, resulting in the carrying off of the produce and the killing of the producers. Such raids were often made by the Navajo on Tusayan, Zuñi, and the eastern pueblos and on the Mexican villages along the Rio Grande for some years after the American occupation, and are continued even today in a small way on the Tusayan. The effect of such raids is cumulative, and it might be several years before important action would result on the part of the village Indians subjected to them. On the other hand, several long seasons might elapse during which comparative immunity would be enjoyed by the village. In the lower Verde there is evidence of two such periods, if not more, and during that time the small pueblos and settlements previously referred to were built. None of these small settlements was occupied, however, for more than a few decades, the ground plans of most of them indicating an even shorter period.

That cavate lodges and cliff-dwellings are simply varieties of the same phase of life, and that life an agricultural one, is a conclusion, supported by the remains in the lower Verde valley. The almost entire absence of cliff-dwellings and the great abundance of cavate lodges has already been commented on, and as the geologic formations are favorable to the latter, and unfavorable to the former on the Verde, whereas the Canyon de Chelly, where there are hundreds of cliff-dwellings and no cavate lodges, the conditions are reversed, this abundance of cavate lodges may be set down as due to an accident of environment. The cavate lodge of the Rio Verde is a more easily constructed and more convenient habitation than the cliff-dwelling of Canyon de Chelly.

An examination and survey of the cliff ruins of Canyon de Chelly, made some years ago by the writer, revealed the fact that they were always located with reference to some area of adjacent tillable land and that the defensive motive exercised so small an influence on the selection of the site and the character of the buildings that it could be ignored. It was found that the cliff-dwellings were merely farming outlooks, and that the villages proper were almost always located on the canyon bottom. With slight modifications these conclusions may be extended over the Verde region and applied to the cavate lodges there. The relation of these lodges to the village ruins and the character of the sites occupied by them support the conclusion that they were farming outlooks, probably occupied only during the farming season, according to the methods followed by many of the Pueblos today, and that the defensive motive had little or no influence on the selection of the site or the character of the structures. The bowlder-marked sites and the small single-room remains illustrate other phases of the same horticultural methods, methods somewhat resembling the "intensive culture," of modern agriculture, but requiring further a close supervision or watching of the crop during the period of ripening. As the area of tillable land in the pueblo region, especially in its western part, is limited, these requirements have developed a class of temporary structures, occupied only during the farming season. In Tusayan, where the most primitive architecture of the pueblo type is found, these structures are generally of brush; in Canyon de Chelly they are cliff-dwellings; on the Rio Verde they are cavate lodges, bowlder-marked sites and single house remains; but at Zuñi they have reached their highest development in the three summer villages of Ojo Caliente, Nutria, and Pescado.

PLATE L. DOORWAY TO CAVATE LODGE.

Since the American occupancy of the country and the consequent removal of the hostile pressure which has kept the Pueblo tribes in check, development has been rapid and now threatens a speedy extinction of pueblo life. The old Laguna has been abandoned, Acoma is being depopulated, the summer pueblos of Zuñi are now occupied all the year round by half a dozen or more families, and even in Tusayan, the most conservative of all the pueblo groups, the abandonment of the home village and location in more convenient single houses has commenced. It is the old process over again, but with the difference that formerly the cycle was completed by the reaggregation of the various families, and little bands into larger groups under hostile pressure from wilder tribes, but now that pressure has been permanently removed, and in a few years, or at most in a few generations, the old pueblo life will be known only by its records.

INDEX

Nutria *27, 100*

O

Of Verde Valley *13*
Ojo Caliente *27, 100*
On Fossil Creek *24*

P

Palat-Kwabi *4*
Pat-Ki-Nyûmû *3*
Pescado *27, 100*
Population Of *13, 47, 68*
Pueblos *3, 10, 12, 13, 14, 16, 17, 18, 23, 24, 31, 32, 39, 46, 53, 54, 57, 68, 82, 96, 97,*
      99, 100, 101

V

Verde Ruins *98*

W

W. J. Hoffman *2*

Lector House believes that a society develops through a two-fold approach of continuous learning and adaptation, which is derived from the study of classic literary works spread across the historic timeline of literature records. Therefore, we aim at reviving, repairing and redeveloping all those inaccessible or damaged but historically as well as culturally important literature across subjects so that the future generations may have an opportunity to study and learn from past works to embark upon a journey of creating a better future.

This book is a result of an effort made by Lector House towards making a contribution to the preservation and repair of original ancient works which might hold historical significance to the approach of continuous learning across subjects.

HAPPY READING & LEARNING!

LECTOR HOUSE LLP
E-MAIL: lectorpublishing@gmail.com